Country Walks in
CONNECTICUT

A Guide to
The Nature Conservancy
Preserves

Second Edition

Susan D. Cooley

Published by
Appalachian Mountain Club Books
and
The Nature Conservancy

Maps by Nora Hennessy Rolston
Cover and text photographs by George Bellerose

Library of Congress Cataloging-in-Publication Data

Cooley, Susan D.
  Country walks in Connecticut / Susan D. Cooley.—2nd ed. p. cm.
  ISBN 0-910146-78-0 (alk. paper)
  1. Walking—Connecticut—Guide-books. 2. Outdoor recreation–
  Connecticut—Guide-books. 3. Connecticut—Description and trav
  el—1981- —Guide-books. I. Appalachian Mountain Club. II. Natur
  Conservancy (U.S.) III. Title.
  GV199.42.C8C66 1989
  917.46'044—dc19   88-3670

Published by Appalachian Mountain Club Books, 5 Joy St., Boston, M/
  02108.
Distributed by The Talman Company, 150 Fifth Ave., New York, N
  10011.

SECOND EDITION

The paper used in this publication meets the minimum requirements of th
American National Standard for Information Sciences—Permanence c
Paper for Printed Library Materials, ANSI Z39.48-1984. ∞

**Due to changes in conditions, use of the
information in this book is at the sole risk
of the user.**

Printed in the United States of America

10 9 8 7 6 5 4   9

For

DR. RICHARD H. GOODWIN

A leader among Conservancy volunteers,
his vision inspired
the Connecticut Chapter's preserve system

TO THE READER

IF YOU FIND any errors in the text or maps, or can suggest improvements, we invite you to send a letter to: Editor, Appalachian Mountain Club Books, 5 Joy St., Boston, MA 02108.

CONTENTS

SHORT HIKES

FOREWORD

THE PUBLICATION OF SUSAN COOLEY'S *Country Walks in Connecticut* brings together two distinguished nonprofit organizations. The Appalachian Mountain Club, founded in 1876, is the nation's oldest mountaineering and conservation group, an international leader in the private management of public recreational lands. The Nature Conservancy, over three decades old, is devoted to preserving land that is ecologically significant. The Conservancy has protected over three million acres in this and other countries, comprising more than a thousand sanctuaries, the largest such preserve system in the world. Both organizations serve the public in innumerable ways, and the present volume testifies to their common purpose in making land accessible to people who seek to participate meaningfully in the natural environment.

Since 1954, the Connecticut Chapter of the Conservancy has protected eighteen thousand acres. Many are owned by the Chapter in over seventy sanctuaries. The rest have been transferred to the state, to municipalities, or to qualified private landholding entities. In all cases, the Conservancy acquires land by private action rather than through public advocacy. Each preserve is dedicated to some public purpose—scientific, educational, or recreational.

The Conservancy's program has three components: identification of critical lands, protection, and stewardship. The process of selecting and designing preserves is based on rational scientific principle. By identifying only those species and biotic communities most likely to vanish, we channel our resources exclusively toward areas acutely in need of protection. We then work within the free-enterprise system to protect land by purchase, gift, bequest, or various other methods. Preserves are managed by local volunteers in cooperation with the Conservancy's professional land stewards.

Twelve thousand of The Nature Conservancy's 450,000 members live in Connecticut. The Chapter is co-managed by a volunteer board of trustees and a small professional staff. A committee of consulting scientists advises on technical matters, and a board of senior business executives promotes land conservation as an object of corporate philanthropy. More than four hundred corporations, including twenty-five in Connecticut, annually support the Conservancy, and many others contribute to capital projects in conservation. The original publication made possible in part by a major grant from Kennecott Corporation—a subsidiary of the Standard Oil Company, Ohio (SOHIO)—and by Aetna Life and Casualty, is but one significant example of how some of the nation's top businesses have taken leadership roles in preserving wilderness for all. In total, American corporations have, over the past few years, contributed millions of dollars and donated thousands of acres of critical habitat, a fact that will surprise many conservationists.

In addition to corporate donations and dues from members, the Conservancy receives gifts of securities, cash, and life insurance, as well as foundation grants and bequests. For every dollar donated to the modest operating budget, sixteen dollars' worth of land is saved in perpetuity.

Connecticut is one of the best-kept secrets on the East Coast. That is both a boon and a problem: a boon because, despite its central location in the Boston–New York megalopolis, much of Connecticut's three-million–acre countryside is rural, nearly pristine, and surpassingly beautiful; a problem because any unknown area—land without a constituency—can fall quickly beneath the bulldozer blade, and no one will be there to prevent it or even, in some cases, to mourn the passing.

Is it appropriate to use the word "mourn" when speaking of natural land that is converted, never to return to original health? I think so, especially if you believe, as does the scientist Aldo Leopold, that people and land are members of a single community of living things. In his brilliant and understated book, *A Sand County Almanac*, Leopold proposes that decent land use is not solely an economic issue. "The first precaution of intelligent tinkering," he wrote, referring to our manner of altering the landscape, "is to save all the parts." The concept of saving the parts evolves from the frightening knowledge that in making over the planet, we are extinguishing species and whole ecosystems at an accelerating rate. This is causing a gross simplification of the earth's biology. Thus, the first reason to save land is to preserve a living resource. Land is the source of all food and most medicines. It is a repository for species and, as such, is the last stronghold of ecological diversity and genetic variation, two safety valves in the struggle for survival of all creatures, including humanity. Land in near-natural condition is a giant sponge for cycling nutrients and for cleaning air and water. The health of *Homo sapiens* and the future of human civilization are directly influenced by the health of the biota.

We do not know, for example, that two of the rare organisms we save at Chapman Pond (a sanctuary described in this book), *Scirpus torreyi* and *Sagittaria montevidensis*—unprepossessing plants with patently unattractive names—might not someday offer a cure for, say, multiple sclerosis. Or that the germs and plasms of another species there, wild rice, will not yield an antidote for an infestation that wants to eradicate whole monocultures of corn or wheat or barley in the American West.

It takes a quantum leap of faith, even for ardent conservationists, to believe that protecting a little chemistry here and there might make life a little better for someone we will never meet. The point is that we just don't know, and so we must err conservatively. You will note that the words "conservation" and "conservative" are variations on a single theme, though they are popularly thought of as politically opposite.

Said differently, if we destroy habitats and species, we destroy present and future sources of food, drugs, clean water, and fresh air, and we diminish in proportion our chances for survival. And that is cause enough to mourn.

Of course, there are many other reasons to protect land, and each represents an important human value—economics, aesthetics, spirituality, education, recreation, or ethics. It is a happy circumstance of the conservation business that these values often overlap. In Connecticut, for example, many of the Conservancy's ecologically important sanctuaries are quite beautiful as well. And in cases in which recreational uses do not compromise the biologic integrity of the preserve, the land can be opened to walking, ski touring, canoeing, and other compatible pleasures. That is the purpose of *Country Walks in Connecticut.*

This book aims to help you explore some lesser-known backcountry around the state. The text has two main sections. The first covers some of the larger preserves, most with established trails. The second discusses other sanctuaries, many trailless or otherwise difficult to access. Many are available to scientists conducting research and to educators and their students. Most preserves are open without prior appointment; others require permission. The Conservancy asks that you respect the restrictions under which each sanctuary is operated.

Mostly, though, we hope that when you explore the land you will enjoy bogs and heaths, mountain summits and ravines, marshlands, rivers, eagles, ospreys, beavers, rare flora, remnant ecosystems, glacial deposits, and talus slopes—all manner of things natural. For they are there for the walking, paddling, and seeing. As you participate in the natural environment, we hope especially that you will pause to consider the meaning of your excursion and will reflect on the fact that as land is converted—particularly on the populous East Coast—the chances decrease for your descendents to have similar experiences.

If that causes you to mourn, it should also impel you to act. Conservation is, in part, the business of mounting dollars and human energies behind selfless goals, such as the maintenance of a beautiful and biologically diverse earth. It is also the hopeful belief that the wealthiest and smartest society the world has yet known can learn to tinker intelligently.

Join The Nature Conservancy, the Appalachian Mountain Club, or any of the other fine organizations that distinguish between standards of living and quality of life. That small commitment will give you immense satisfaction and will yield real hope that some species and habitats can be saved. And that is cause enough for joy.

W. Kent Olson
president, American Rivers
past executive director, The Nature Conservancy,
Connecticut Chapter

PREFACE

WHEN WAS THE LAST TIME YOU EXPLORED a Nature Conservancy preserve? Or perhaps you have never experienced the excitement and exhilaration that come with your first visit to one of the thousand Nature Conservancy preserves nationwide. Chances are there is a preserve near your home, and *Country Walks in Connecticut* by Susan D. Cooley is your ticket to some of the best performances nature has to offer in the Nutmeg State.

First published by the Appalachian Mountain Club and the Connecticut Chapter of The Nature Conservancy in 1982, *Country Walks* was such an overwhelming success that it quickly went through two printings. Before printing a second edition, we asked Susan to update the book and add a few newly acquired Conservancy preserves. The result is an even more useful guide to a selection of The Nature Conservancy's uncrowded and undisturbed natural treasures in Connecticut.

Our state is resplendent with biological diversity and ecological richness. But as development ripples across our landscape, many of our unique natural habitats are being destroyed. If not for the leadership and vision of a handful of Connecticut's leading conservationists, the Conservancy preserves described in this guide would not exist today. In 1960, an assemblage of Conservancy members, organized by Dr. William Niering and Dr. Richard Goodwin, gathered in Osborne Laboratory at Yale University to charter the Connecticut Chapter of The Nature Conservancy. The Chapter's mission is to identify, preserve, and manage Connecticut's most significant natural lands. For nearly three decades The Nature Conservancy has been building a living legacy of over seventy-one wild and unspoiled preserves. This incredible sanctuary system was assembled through the dedication, hard work, and generosity of thousands of Conservancy members and donors. Each and every person associated with The Nature Conservancy can be proud of this legacy.

Throughout our lives, experiences with nature revitalize our spirits and keep us in touch with our world. It is exciting to be alive and to experience nature first-hand. *Country Walks* will introduce you to such experiences; so put on your hiking shoes, pack a lunch, and get out the door to explore these slices of Connecticut's natural heritage. Your curiosity and sense of adventure are bound to be piqued by Susan's enticing style. She has bushwhacked, climbed, and paddled her way across Connecticut to bring you this menu of Conservancy entrees. She has squeezed thousands of acres and miles of trails into this compact field guide. The text and maps are well organized, selective, and interpretive, and all are solidly grounded in years of field experience. This guidebook will inspire you to go out and explore some of what The Nature Conservancy has worked so diligently to save. And best of all, you can return home feeling secure in your memories, for The Nature Conservancy will continue to serve as steward and guardian over these wild areas so that their biological bounty and natural splendor will be there for future generations to enjoy.

When you visit a Conservancy preserve, please remember to leave only footprints and to take only photographs and memories.

Leslie N. Corey, Jr.
executive director, The Nature Conservancy,
Connecticut Chapter

ACKNOWLEDGMENTS

BECAUSE OF THE ENORMOUS SUCCESS of *Country Walks in Connecticut* I was asked to update and revise the guidebook for a second edition. The process of revision has been gratifying. It has given me the incentive to revisit most of The Nature Conservancy's holdings in the state, which is pleasurable in itself. These visits have also been a forceful reminder of the importance of the Conservancy's work in providing lasting protection for thousands of acres of Connecticut's most critical natural areas.

On a personal level, working on the guidebook at the Conservancy's Connecticut Chapter in Middletown, where I spent many years on staff, has been like a prolonged family reunion with my friends and colleagues there. Beth Lapin, the Science and Stewardship Director, and her assistant, Rachel Aptekar, were most helpful in reading the manuscript and offering useful criticism.

The extended Conservancy family includes the many volunteers who keep an eye on the nature sanctuaries, and whose years of observation have been incorporated in this book. Members of the local stewardship committees read sections of my original manuscript, and I want to thank them for their time and comments. Thanks also to Lauren Brown and Julie Zickefoose for critically reading portions of the original work, and to Ken Olson for reading every last word and giving constant encouragement.

This reunion also includes my friends George Bellerose, the talented photographer, and Nora Hennessy Rolston, the able cartographer. The book's revision gave us the good excuse to work together again, and their work greatly enriches this volume.

The guidebook revision has caused other positive entanglements, most notably with the sterling Simsbury Secretarial Service under the competent direction of Joan Roemer. It was there that I met Mary Gridley, who tirelessly typed and retyped the entire manuscript, offered good editorial comment, and conquered the recalcitrant *italics* on her stubborn computer. The book's legibility is a credit to her skill and good humor.

Country Walks was originally made possible by major grants from the Aetna Life and Casualty Company, Ensworth Charitable Foundation Trust, and Kennecott Corporation, a subsidiary of the Standard Oil Company (SOHIO).

Finally, that I was allowed time off to revise the guidebook is due to a most understanding employer, Austin Dunham Barney II, president of Farmvest, Inc., in Simsbury. His commitment to land preservation, be it farmland or wild land, was sorely tested during this revision, and I thank him for his patience.

Susan D. Cooley

INTRODUCTION

MANY VISITORS TO CONNECTICUT see the state only superficially, glimpsing it from a car window as they speed by the urbanized landscape adjacent to Interstate 95. Slow down and take the back roads! Connecticut has lots more to offer, including a diversity of terrain that is still quite wild in character and gives the hiker a sense of being far from city crowds.

Country Walks in Connecticut highlights nineteen walks and five canoe trips that one can take on The Nature Conservancy's natural area sanctuaries in Connecticut. The book also briefly describes some other holdings of this organization. These parcels will be protected forever, and all told represent an array of landscapes typically found in the state.

Connecticut's coast is characterized by low-lying land and sandy beaches intermixed with rocky headlands extending into Long Island Sound (Griswold Point). The coastal zone includes estuaries and tidal marshes where ospreys nest and ducks and herons feed (Great Island Marsh, and Pattagansett Marshes).

The lower Connecticut River Valley is especially picturesque, and is a vital habitat for young shellfish and fin fish. At Middletown, the river swings southeastward, cuts through the eastern highlands, and flows past rugged hills (Chapman Pond) and broad flood-plain forests of silver maple and cottonwood (Lord Cove).

Connecticut's central lowland is underlain by Triassic sedimentary bedrock characterized by reddish-brown sandstones. Delineating the landscape is a series of resistant basalt, or trap-rock, ridges that rise several hundred feet above the valley floor (Higby Mountain). Their well-drained soils support hemlock and central hardwoods, dominated by oaks and hickories.

To either side of the central lowlands lie more resistant highlands that are underlain primarily by metamorphosed gneisses and schists. In Salisbury and Norfolk, in the far northwestern corner of the state, lies the highest and most rugged terrain, the southern extension of the Berkshire Mountains. These uplands support white pine, hemlock, and northern hardwoods—sugar maple, black cherry, white ash, and paper birch (Hamlet Hill). In these northern swamps and bogs, northern species of hardwoods reach the southernmost limit of their range (Phelps Research Area and Walcott Preserve, which are off-limits).

The northwest uplands, along the Housatonic River and in Litchfield, are at a slightly lower elevation and enjoy a milder climate. Here transitional hardwoods occur, dominated by representtive species from both northern hardwoods—sugar maple, black birch, white ash—and central hardwoods—oaks and hickories (Buell Natural Area, Cathedral Pines, Iron Mountain Reservation, St. Johns Ledges). These uplands are interspersed with steep-walled valleys whose metamorphosed limestone bedrock enriches the overlying soils. The soils, in turn, support a splendid array of plants.

The northwest hills have an even milder climate reflected in a somewhat more southerly vegetation association of central hardwoods and white pines (Barnes Memorial Nature Preserve and Buttermilk Falls). In eastern Connecticut, the highlands are characterized by the same high plateaus into which broad valleys are incised (Dennis Farm Preserve and Rock Spring).

Within about twenty-five miles of the coast lie the southern hills. They reach moderate elevations (250 to 750 feet) with bedrock outcrops. Central hardwoods are the major forest vegetation, with the tulip tree, a more southern species, an important feature of lower slopes and wetland edges (Burnham Brook, Devil's Den, Milo Light Preserve, and Weir Preserve).

While each ecoregion[1] of the state is quite distinct, the hiker can look for recurring patterns of vegetation composition within a given natural area. Across Connecticut, ridgetops tend to be harsh environments, buffeted by drying winds and covered in thin, excessively drained soils. The lack of available moisture may produce stunted growth in the relatively few species that tolerate the severe conditions, for example, the chestnut oak, with huckleberry or low blueberry as ground cover.

Farther downhill, on the midslope, the site conditions are generally such that the soils are deeper, moister, and more enriched by whatever nutrients are brought downhill by runoff. Here the sugar maple, ash, and paper birch grow well in the northernmost part of the state, while oaks and hickories flourish in central and southern Connecticut. Beech trees very often occur on the midslope, especially on hills with a western aspect. The shrub layer is frequently a mixture of maple-leaved viburnum, witch hazel, and mountain laurel.

The lower slopes, still elevated above the poorly drained wetlands, tend to be the richest sites of the forest because of the nutrient runoff. Here tulip trees (south) and basswood (north) do well. In cooler pockets, or on north-facing slopes, the hemlock and yellow birch thrive. The moisture may favor spicebush and sweet pepperbush in the shrub layer, with a variety of ferns forming a ground cover.

The wetlands, if open, will most likely produce tussock sedge, blue flag, and cattails; if shrubby, alders and willows

---

[1] J. Dowhan and R. Craig, *Rare and Endangered Species of Connecticut and Their Habitats*. Report of Investigations No. 6 (Hartford, CT: Department of Environmental Protection, 1976).

will dominate; and if wooded, one is certain to find red maples. Skunk cabbage and false hellebore will occur on the poorly drained, mucky soils of wetlands and along watercourses.

Connecticut, situated in a transitional zone between northern and central forest types, produces different "pioneer" species on abandoned fields. In northern Connecticut, white pine seeds in readily on old fields. It is fairly common to find even-aged pine stands neatly confined within stone-wall boundaries that once served to keep cows in. Farther south, long-abandoned fields are invaded by the red cedar, whose seed germinates well in thick sod.

Such a brief primer, of course, gives a simplistic view of the landscape, and there are many exceptions to the rules stated above. However, Nature does repeat herself, and a few pointers on what to look for in each region of Connecticut may help hikers and canoeists enjoy themselves while visiting the Conservancy's sanctuaries.

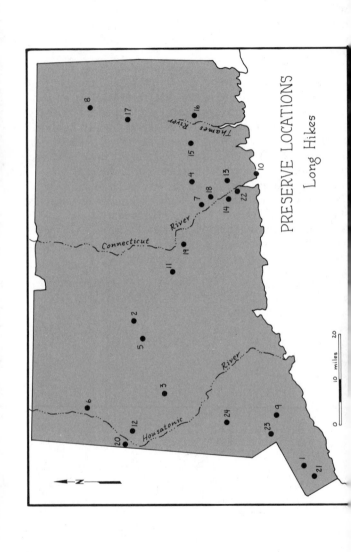

PRESERVE LOCATIONS
Long Hikes

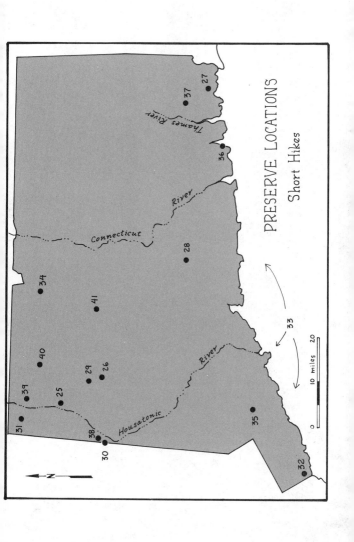

PRESERVE LOCATIONS
Short Hikes

1

ALTSCHUL PRESERVE

Stamford

*Walking—Approximately 1.5 miles through a
mature oak forest and across the East Branch of the
Mianus River. This preserve is a very valuable parcel
of open space in an increasingly urbanized area.*

---

*DIRECTIONS: From the Merritt Parkway, take exit
34 and go north on Route 104. In 2.3 miles turn
left (through two stone pillars) on Sawmill Road. Go
0.7 mile and turn left on Dundee Road. The preserve
lies to the right in 0.5 mile. Park by the side of the
road.*

THE TERRAIN OF THIS 163-acre preserve is typical
of the upland found in Greenwich and Stamford. The
remarkably rough ground is actually eroded mountain
peaks whose valleys now lie far under Long Island
Sound. The valleys filled with glacial meltwater about
twelve thousand years ago as the Wisconsin Glacier, the
last in a series of glaciers to cover New England, receded.
The terminal moraine of this glacier formed Long Island.
As the glacier continued to shrink northward, it left rock
ridges exposed and covered slopes and lowlands with
glacial till (an assortment of rocks, cobbles, sand, and silt).

The watercourses of southwestern Connecticut, such as the Mianus River, continue to drain these uplands of Stamford and Greenwich and to carry rich sediments downstream to nourish the vegetation of the flood plains.

Take the trail leading from the road and follow it along the northern boundary, thereby skirting the small wetland. Continue along the eastern shoulder of a rise and proceed directly west along the well-used trail to the bridge across the East Branch of the Mianus River.

In spring, the peepers provide music for most of the hike. The vernal pool at the northeast corner of the preserve is an important breeding site for frogs and salamanders, and bubbles with life in April and May. By midsummer, however, the standing water observed in spring has disappeared, having evaporated or dropped with the water table below the surface of the ground. The vegetation is typical of wetlands. Yellow birch and tulip trees occupy the edge of moist areas, while spicebush, skunk cabbage, and a variety of fern species thrive throughout the depression.

When the trail rises slightly, wetland tree species drop out, and black, red, and white oaks increase in number as canopy trees. Dogwoods dominate the understory on the midslope, yielding to thick stands of laurel on the well-drained higher elevations. The trail lies between spectacular rocky cliffs of granite gneiss which are worth exploring. To the south of the trail an overhang forms caves, and a north–south fracture creates a natural tunnel.

There are many dead oaks along the well-drained hilltops—casualties of gypsy moth defoliation compounded by too little rainfall over the past decade. Standing dead trees are an important component of any forest because

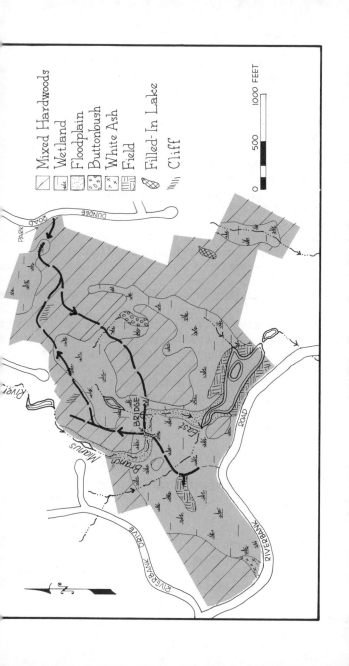

Mixed Hardwoods
Wetland
Floodplain
Buttonbush
White Ash
Field
Filled-In Lake
Cliff

0   500   1000 FEET

DUNDEE ROAD
PARK ROAD
Mianus River
Branch
East
BRIDGE
RIVERBANK DRIVE
RIVERBANK ROAD

N

they provide food and shelter for a variety of creatures. Unfortunately, in our present economy, wood for fuel is at a premium. Standing dead trees, although they yield comparatively little heat, are felled first because they are dry and ready for the stove. A forest depleted of standing dead trees quickly loses its woodpecker, opossum, and flying squirrel populations. The dead oaks on this preserve offer an ample habitat for such residents.

The west-facing slope above the river appears to have been cleared during colonial times, perhaps for grazing because so many surface stones remain. Early successional species, those that appear in the succession toward reforestation, have grown up here in full sunlight and include greenbrier, red cedar, and hay-scented fern.

During winter, atop a snow cover, or in early spring, among the leaves, look for a perfectly common sight— jet black springtails or snow fleas. These curious, minute creatures are a primitive type of insect, or Collembolid. They can withstand freezing temperatures and are found almost everywhere, including the Antarctic. Often they are first heard peppering the dry leaves as they spring about. They may also appear in a tightly packed platoon forming a thick, felty mass with a metallic sheen. This extraordinary swarm moves across the ground, probably feeding or mating.

At the bridge over the East Branch, consider a brief side trip to the other side of the river. An old road leads out to Riverbank Road past a flood-plain forest and a dump.

There is a low, flat area of almost three acres situated between the two branches of the river. The alluvial soils here support a "monoculture" of young red maple sprouts. Shrubs are conspicuously absent, although tussock sedge grows in profusion. This area, probably once cleared and planted in hay or crops, is periodically flooded. Look for long-fingered raccoon prints in pockets of soft mud.

Beyond the flat area on the right-hand side of the old road lies an elevated area. Long a local dump, it is now overgrown with blackberries and sumac. In the past ten years access from Riverbank Road was blocked, and there has been no further dumping, but the area remains an eyesore and a source of concern for the local steward-ship committee. Cleanup parties have been formed from time to time, but removing the larger debris would require heavy and costly equipment.

Return to the bridge, bear left, and follow the old road uphill along the stone wall. After 600 feet, turn right on a well-worn trail that leads to a large rock outcrop.

You may have to duck under a large fallen tree barring the way. Use caution! The hairy rope-like vine is poison ivy, still thriving, and should be avoided. Poison ivy, like bittersweet and grapevines, is a kind of mild parasite that lacks the ability to grow tall without support. Poison ivy climbs trees and shrubs by clinging with its hairy holdfasts; bittersweet coils about its host plant; grapevines attach themselves to a sapling and, as the tree grows, they hitchhike upward. All three plants ultimately reach the canopy where they may be so successful in competing for sunlight that they completely shade out their host trees, which then die. Observe the huge grapevines across the stone wall. They are probably the approximate age of the surrounding forest.

The top of the hill adjacent to the cul-de-sac of Mill-stream Road had become the playground of local teen-age trail bikers, but the preserve committee has dealt squarely with these violators of the Altschul Preserve, and their activities have abated.

The trail, dipping to the right of an enormous outcrop, follows the edge of a wetland along the preserve's northeastern boundary to a trail running east–west. Turn right (east) and proceed until you join the main trail. Bear left and continue to your car.

The trail skirting the wetland joins the east–west trail at a small aspen grove. Aspen trees are an early successional species that invades old fields and, once established, may reproduce via root suckers. When the genetic material of an entire grove is identical, one speaks of aspen "clones."

The last section of the east–west trail before the junction with the main trail follows fairly level ground, with high outcrop summits rising fifteen to thirty feet above the trail. The woods are dominated by mature oaks.

Land for the preserve was donated to the Conservancy by Helen G. Altschul in 1975 and 1977, and by John J. McCloy in 1977.

2

BARNES MEMORIAL NATURE PRESERVE

Bristol

Visiting museum and walking—Ideal for children. Educational displays are on view in the museum. The walk boasts a variety of terrain and trail: stream edges, bridges, boardwalks across swamps, mountain-laurel tunnels, a steep hill over a glacial esker with a view, and an open field. Plan to spend a couple of hours. There is no picnicking, and pets are not allowed.

DIRECTIONS: From Route 6 in Bristol go north on Route 69 for 2 miles. Go right on Shrub Road. The Harry C. Barnes Memorial Nature Preserve and the Nature Center's parking lot are located 2000 feet down the road on the north (left) side.

THE NATURE CENTER HOUSES various natural-history displays and a small nature library. During the week, there are ecology classes for school children. The center is open weekdays, except Monday. The weekend schedule is variable, so it's best to telephone ahead of time (203-589-6082). The trails are open every day from dawn till dusk.

Before leaving the museum, check the bird feeders to see what seed eaters may be in the area. Directly behind the building is a tiny pond with its share of frogs. The pond was dug when the center was constructed in 1972, and cattails are filling it in.

Follow the red-blazed trail leading to the right (east) of the center and around a red-maple swamp. The footing is uneven and there are many exposed roots, so watch your step.

The drier margins of the wetland were formerly cleared and grazed. Keep an eye out for tree species that inhabit fields. You will see old apple trees and red cedars now topped by black birches and large white pines. Many of the pines have double or triple trunks, most probably the result of the white pine weevil. The weevil will kill the terminal shoot of a young pine growing in full sunlight and alter the tree's straight growth pattern. One or more of the topmost lateral branches compete for the lead and cause either a single crook or multiple stems.

The trail passes from the woods to the edge of Falls Brook. Follow the trail upstream leaving the brook on your right.

Both stream banks are hidden in thick mountain laurel. The trail is wonderfully cut through these thickets and is always within earshot of running water. A child can camper through this winding tunnel, but adults will have a slower time of it. Large yellow birches growing along the stream are generally considered a more northern species and are an important component of the northern

 Field		• Nature Center	
Red Maple		⬏ Overlook	
Birch/Maple		▥ Footbridge	
Oak/Hickory			

0   500   1000   1500 FEET

mixed-hardwood forest. They are able to thrive here because the microclimate of the stream valley is cooler and damper than the surrounding area.

The red-blazed trail leads to a bridge over Falls Brook. Cross over the bridge and continue upstream through more laurel. Turn left at the T and continue until you reach a second bridge at a wide bend in the stream. Do not cross here, but follow the yellow-blazed trail straight ahead. In a short distance the path bears away from the stream and begins a steep ascent up Pigeon Hill.

Climbing the hill, the hiker follows a moisture gradient that plays an important role in limiting vegetation growth. The yellow birch and red maple are left in the cool moist lowland, and are replaced by hemlocks as the soils become better drained on the lower slopes. The hemlock became established here because of a single seed source: the large parent hemlock, now dead, located to the left of the trail. Farther upslope, on excessively drained droughty soils, are the oaks. Red, black, and white oaks tolerate drier soils than maples and birches do. However, because of the repeated heavy infestation by gypsy moth caterpillars (on ridge sites in particular), these oaks may have trouble over the next few years.

The barbed wire embedded in the trees to the north of the trail, running from the wetland to the top of the ridge, is testimony that even this steep slope was once grazed.

As your heart pounds with the exertion of this climb, consider that you are ascending an esker that formed as the last glacier melted some twelve thousand years ago. Meltwater streams within the glacier were confined by walls of ice, and these winding channels slowly filled with layered sand, pebbles, and stones to form this sinuous ridge.

Once at the top of the Pigeon Hill esker, take a side trip to see the gravel pits and Mine Mountain to the north. Follow the yellow blazes east (right) for several hundred feet. The mining of sand and gravel on the north-facing slope that falls away at your feet ceased more than a decade ago. Now the only disturbance in the area comes from motorcycles and trail bikes. For the most part, these bikes keep to the pits and avoid the Nature Center's trails, but the noise is irritating.

Since the gravel pits closed, the slopes have stabilized and vegetation has adapted to the sterile site. Tufts of little bluestem grass have taken hold along with sweet fern. Beside the trail are huckleberry, azalea, and mountain laurel. The gray birch tolerates this site, as does pitch pine intermixed with white pine. The trees growing along the ridge are almost all white oaks and quite dwarfed in size, probably due to the exposed site and the excessively drained soils.

Although the yellow trail continues southward and rejoins the red trail, we suggest you return along the same path and continue northwest along the ridge, following the green blazes. The trail proceeds through a stand of pitch pine.

The droughty soils of the esker are typical of pitch pine sites. In Connecticut, pitch pine is found on the few existing sandy outwash plains, more typical of New Jersey and Cape Cod, and on sandy or rocky geologic features, such as eskers, exposed to the drying winds. Pitch pine is known as a "fire-adaptive" species. It grows on excessively dry terrain that is subject to sweeping fires. Over the millennia, the species has developed a thick, tough bark that can withstand burning temperatures. Fire-damaged pitch pines occasionally sprout, a rarity among conifers. Furthermore, some pitch pine cones will not release their seeds unless a fire's heat triggers their scales to open.

In winter, the views to the southwest extend over the wetland. The woods are mature and the trees well spaced, giving a park-like effect. On sunny days when snow is on the ground the patterns of animal tracks and birch catkins are visible, and nuthatches and chickadees sing overhead.

The Barnes Nature Preserve is a small island surrounded by urban growth. It probably provides as much "wilderness" as some of the Bristol-area schoolchildren will ever experience. Fortunately, the Nature Center is active in environmental education, and offers the students and their parents a variety of natural-history classes.

The trail comes to an obvious old road-cut (natural or man-made) that leads downhill. Continue along the ridge trail about 100 feet and look for a green blaze pointing downhill through mountain laurel.

This south-facing slope supports sizable oaks which, situated midslope, benefit from increased runoff and the nutrients brought downslope. Better protected in the lee of the ridge and warmed by increased sunlight (given the southern exposure), these oaks grow larger than the ones occupying the dry, windy summit. Black birches are numerous, and mountain laurel also thrives in this richer site.

The trail, dipping gently across the slope, drops at last to the valley floor. It continues across the wetland via a series of boardwalks (some in poor repair) to a bridge across Falls Brook, where it joins a connector trail leading to the Connecticut Tunxis Trail.

The oaks of the midslope give way to species that require greater moisture. The trail enters the wetland at the foot of several towering, arrow-straight tulip trees (or yellow poplars). Not a true poplar, but a member of the magnolia family, the tulip tree grows very rapidly and its wood is prized for cabinet work. Where cultivated for timber, tulip trees may be cut on rotations of forty years or less. Nearing their northern limits here in Connecticut they are quite susceptible to flooding and fire. Once in the wetland, the dominant groundcover is cinnamon fern with its fuzzy-stemmed fronds. Spicebushes (crush a leaf and smell it), with their speckled bark, form the shrub stratum while large red maples and yellow birches dominate the forest canopy.

A few hundred feet downstream from the bridge (beside a wooden crossing), notice the overturned red maple. Apparently undermined by high water and subsequent wind, the shallow root system could no longer support the tree and it toppled into the stream. A lush growth of grass has since established itself on the root ball.

Once at the Tunxis Trail, turn south (left) and follow Falls Brook downstream. The trail leads through the woods, past a field, and back toward the Nature Center parking lot.

The Connecticut Blue Trail System has a distinguished half-century history. Planned and maintained by the Trail Committee and numerous volunteers of the Connecticut Forest and Park Association, the Blue Trails crisscross the entire state. If you turned north (right), this leg of the Blue Trail, the Tunxis Trail, would lead you to Sessions Woods in Burlington, and on to the Mattatuck Trail at Buttermilk Falls in Plymouth (see Chapter 5).

Once it leaves the stream-side, the trail rises into an oak and hickory forest. The climb is abrupt, and runs over an ancient river terrace formed by the same glacial outwash that created the esker on the far side of the valley.

The large, multistemmed hardwoods are the result of past logging activities. The trees were cut seventy or eighty years ago, and the stumps sprouted. Many slim sprouts bristled from the edge of each stump and competed for light, so only very few grew to maturity. These two or three surviving stems grew quite rapidly, since the mature roots of the severed stump accelerated their growth.

The final few hundred feet of trail pass a mown field. Notice the "islands" of rock, trees, and shrubs, and take a moment to inspect the one closest to the trail. The twisted black cherry trees are in poor health because they are covered in bittersweet and poison ivy. These vines are parasites that use the trees to support their growth and block the light from most of the trees' leaves.

Under the spreading branches of the trees, where the mower cannot reach, grows a variety of woody shrubs. Blackberry, barberry, greenbrier, and rose bushes dominate the area—all with thorns and a ready ability to spread by runners. Herbaceous plants in this area include little bluestem and orchard grass, evening primrose, and goldenrod.

The Center hays this field, and the harvest helps support the farm animals at the Center's Indian Rock Preserve and farm. At the same time, the mowing maintains additional diverse habitat.

There is a short self-guided nature trail behind the Nature Center; a companion guide is available from the Center. The loop trail is blazed in white and has informative signs posted at trail attractions.

Forty acres of the Barnes Memorial Nature Preserve were donated to the Conservancy by Mrs. Harry C.

Barnes in 1970. Twenty-seven acres were purchased from Adrian and Charles Matthews in 1974. Eighty-seven acres of nearby farm and woodland were willed to the Conservancy by Katharine Shepard in 1987. Although not adjacent to the Barnes Preserve, the Barnes Nature Center manages the land.

3

BELLAMY PRESERVE

Bethlehem

Walking—A mile or so of level walking through post-agricultural land now grown to mixed hardwoods or purposefully planted to conifers and nut and fruit trees.

DIRECTIONS: From the north or south, take Route 6 to Bethlehem. From the east or west, take Route 132 to Bethlehem. At the junction of Routes 132 and 61, go west on Route 132 (also known as West Road). Take the first right (north) on Munger Lane and pull into the first driveway on the right, where you will see a preserve sign. Park to one side of this access road.

THE BELLAMY PRESERVE is a ninety-acre tract in the center of Bethlehem and, as such, provides lasting protection of the town's rural flavor. It lies just to the north of the donor's private residence which must be respected. The local Bethlehem Land Trust members maintain this property.

Go through the gate across the access road, continue uphill, and take the path on your left which

*cuts diagonally across the lot with the pond. This
path passes by a huge ash tree with a bench beneath
it, and wanders in a northerly direction to eventually
meet the old stone-lined lane that runs the length of
the preserve.*

This first "old field" is now largely grown to mature
white pine and European larch. There are also cultivated
shrubs, such as the lilacs and forsythias that surround the
small man-made pond. In early autumn the paths are
flanked with asters—both white and lavender—and
goldenrod, making the walk an especially pretty one. The
pond is occasionally "harvested" (cleaned of a percentage
of its weeds) in order to keep the surface waters clear.
In most Conservancy preserves nature is allowed to
take her course. Not so at Bellamy, which is managed
more intensively, in keeping with its historic character as
manipulated farmland.

The second "old field," separated by a stone wall from
the first, has been left to revert back to woods quite naturally. Immediately noticeable are the handsome northern
red-oak trees with straight, well-formed trunks which
dominate the mixed hardwoods.

Some dozen years ago, an effort was made to underplant
these canopy trees with hemlocks, to add variety to the
forest. Hemlock trees tolerate deep shade, growing very
slowly. As holes open naturally in the upper story of
the forest, hemlocks take advantage of the light and
are "released" and grow moderately fast. Unfortunately
for these young trees, the gypsy moths and their larvae
arrived and, having stripped the deciduous trees bare,
the caterpillars descended on the hemlock. The results
were devastating: while deciduous trees have the ability to leaf out after such an infestation, conifers do
not. Without needles, these trees cannot feed themselves and soon die. Notice the misty hue that the

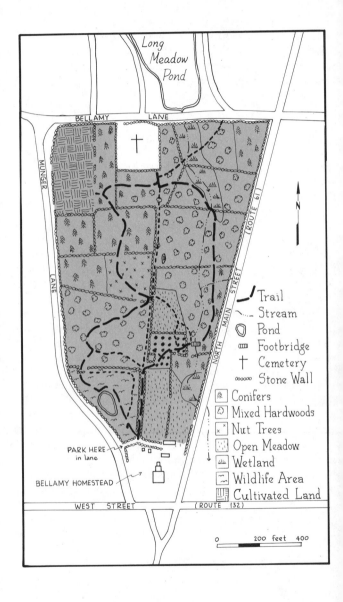

Long Meadow Pond

BELLAMY LANE

MUNGER LANE

NORTH MAIN STREET (ROUTE 61)

N

Trail
Stream
Pond
Footbridge
Cemetery
Stone Wall

Conifers
Mixed Hardwoods
Nut Trees
Open Meadow
Wetland
Wildlife Area
Cultivated Land

PARK HERE in lane

BELLAMY HOMESTEAD

WEST STREET (ROUTE 132)

0   200 feet   400

grey stubs of the doomed hemlock give the shrub layer.

*The path emerges on the old lane where the broad
stone walls have been recently repaired. Squeeze past
the split-rail fence and continue on the path in
a northerly direction through an overgrown field of
three- to six-foot-tall black walnut trees, leaving the
old lane to your right. Continue on this path
through the next "old fields" of conifers and mixed
hardwoods until you reach a small cemetery.*

The black walnut trees are growing reluctantly. They were originally planted as an income-producing project: a single, well-formed mature black walnut tree sold commercially can bring several thousand dollars. Its heavy, dark wood is much sought-after for veneers, cabinetry, and gunstocks. Indeed, this species has been almost entirely cut from the forest in certain regions of the United States. Accordingly, the Bellamy management plan treats these potential gold bars with special care, and members of the stewardship committee periodically trim around the saplings.

The next field to the north, neatly surrounded by stone walls, was planted half to Norway spruce (west side) and half to red pine (east side). The path once led between the two species, but several years back the red pine was salvage-cut and sold before it was killed by a naturally occurring fungus. This disease would have ruined the pine as a commercial log and allowed the spread of disease to neighboring plantations.

An opportunistic plant—the grapevine—was quick to cover the unsightly red-pine slash following the cut. Typically, grapevines move horizontally—over the lower woody plants that poke through the slash—and claim most of the sunlight. As these young trees grow, the grapevine gets a free ride upwards and steals more and more sunlight, eventually killing the host trees. Ultimately, the trees' limbs crumble, and both tree and vine fall to the ground.

The most northerly section of the Bellamy Preserve supports mixed hardwoods and white pine. The soils are moister here and support shrubs, such as spicebush with its pungent leaves. There are areas of thick hay-scented fern and sarsaparilla, and (beware!) a heavy carpet of poison ivy, easily distinguishable by its clusters of three shiny leaves along a running vine.

Once at the cemetery, whose graves date from the 1770s, retrace your steps for a hundred feet. If you've run out of time and wish to go directly back to your car, you can proceed south down the old lane. If you're game for another fifteen minutes, take the trail leading to your left (east) which, in a hundred feet, leads you through one stone wall and across a streambed via another stone wall. Continue south to another stream-crossing via a simple footbridge. Keeping the open field on your left, proceed straight uphill, out along branching trails, and through an overgrown apple orchard to the old lane. Turn left on the old lane and return to your car.

The homeward journey is through mixed hardwoods and a cool hemlock grove. Notice the very spongy-looking sphagnum moss at the stone-wall crossing and the extensive ground cover of clubmosses. At the northwest corner of the first hay field keep a lookout for a sizable American chestnut sprout. It perseveres, still nurtured by the original rootstock whose main trunk died around 1910.

The last leg of the trail runs along a stone wall where bluebird boxes are erected. As many as eight pair of bluebirds have nested at Bellamy in the past few years with good fledging success.

The preserve is leased to The Nature Conservancy by its owner, Miss Caroline Ferriday.

4

BURNHAM BROOK

East Haddam

Walking—A hilly 1.5 miles through post-agricultural oak and hickory forests and along Burnham Brook as it flows through a hemlock ravine. It is a gentle climb over a rock slide to the crest of the ridge. The loop trip provides excellent birding.

DIRECTIONS: From the north: Follow Route 2 and then Route 11; exit at Witch Meadow Road, and turn right at the bottom of the ramp. Go 0.5 mile on Witch Meadow Road, then turn left onto West Road and continue 3 miles to Dolbia Hill Road (second right). The entrance is 0.5 mile up Dolbia Hill Road on the right.

From the west: Follow I-95 to Old Lyme, exit 70. Turn left at the bottom of the ramp onto Route 156 and continue about 9 miles to its end. Turn right onto Route 82 and continue for 2.5 miles until you reach Woodbridge Road. Turn left and proceed 1 mile, then turn left onto Dolbia Hill Road. The entrance is on the right in 0.5 mile.

From the east: Follow I-95 to exit 77; turn right onto Route 85 and continue about 10 miles to the traffic light at Route 82. Turn left on Route 82 and go 2.3 miles. When you reach Woodbridge Road turn

right and drive for 1 mile. Turn left onto Dolbia Hill Road; the entrance is on the right in 0.5 mile.

ENCOMPASSING A MAJOR PART of the Burnham Brook Watershed, the preserve at Burnham Brook is of special interest to field researchers. Preliminary studies of the natural resources reveal good variety in the wildlife on the preserve. The vegetation inventory to date includes over a hundred species of trees, shrubs, and vines; better than 380 herbaceous flowering plants; and more than thirty species of ferns, clubmosses, and horsetails. Records of blooming dates have been kept for the past thirty years. In addition, there is a wealth of mosses, liverworts, lichens, and literally hundreds of fungi.

Also included in the preserve's inventory are more than sixty total species of mammals, reptiles, amphibians, and fish. About 180 species of birds have been sighted on the preserve, and the stewardship committee has undertaken several censuses of those that are breeding. Recently, the Yale Medical School has been using this natural area to further its research on Lyme disease, which is now known to be spread via ticks that prey on native mammals. Seven species of ticks and fifteen species of mosquitoes were collected during this investigation!

This 491-acre preserve is used primarily for field research, so visitors are requested to stay on the marked trail described below in order to avoid interfering with any ongoing studies.

Climb through the log barway at the entrance and follow the old lane downhill to the register. Please sign in. The trail is sparsely, though adequately, blazed with small light-blue rectangular markers placed at intersections and turns. Two vertical markers indicate a turn in the direction of the lower

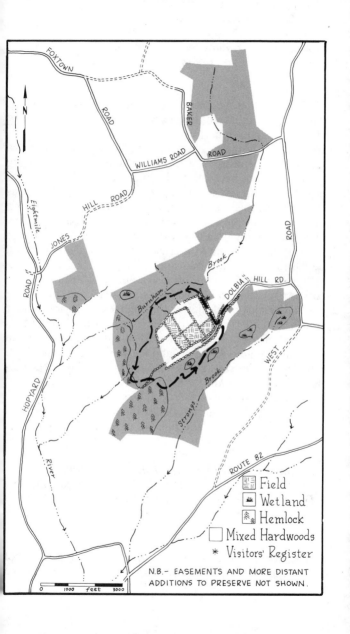

FOXTOWN

ROAD

BAKER

WILLIAMS ROAD   ROAD

HILL   ROAD

Eightmile

JONES

ROAD

Burnham   Brook

DOLBIA   HILL RD.

ROAD

HOPYARD

Strongs   Brook

WEST

River

ROUTE 82

🏫 Field
🌿 Wetland
🌲 Hemlock
☐ Mixed Hardwoods
✳ Visitors' Register

N.B.– EASEMENTS AND MORE DISTANT
ADDITIONS TO PRESERVE NOT SHOWN.

0   1000   feet   3000

mark. Another mark farther along the trail will give assurance that you are on the right track.

In descending the path, you followed an old farm road, flanked by parallel stone walls with a series of log barways, all but one long since gone, opening to the adjacent fields. In the past, this narrow way allowed farm animals to move between two pastures without harming crops or mixing with other pastured livestock. In places, the roadbed has now filled with hay-scented fern which, with its tenacious runners, has covered wide expanses of land to the exclusion of other herbaceous species. In summer, the path is aglow in a pale, yellow-green light that by early autumn turns to a tawny hue. Should you crush a frond in passing, you'll delight in its delicate fragrance.

To the right of the preserve-sign and register-box lies the corner of a stone wall piled high with smaller cobbles. East Haddam's rocky soil, derived from glacial till, yields more stones than are required to build a broad stone wall. To rid the land of rock, a farmer would pile the larger stones in a row to create a fence around the perimeter of the field. Smaller cobbles could be tossed out of the way in the corners. There is another pile of this type by the barway at the entrance to the preserve. Over the years, some organic material has accumulated in these rock piles, and now Virginia creeper and haircap moss are taking hold.

Continue downhill past the corner of the stone wall on your left. A blue blaze leads you farther downhill. The trail soon swings to the left (west) and parallels the slope's contour.

The northwest-facing slope supports a young forest of oaks and red maples, with occasional ironwoods in the understory. The forest floor is covered with clubmoss, which often indicates past grazing on a site. Gray birch trees, which first invaded the pasture, died out about twenty-five years ago.

The trail crosses a small gully fed by Copperhead Spring. The gully remains mucky most of the year and flows only intermittently.

Shortly after the gully, look for a pair of blazes that lead downhill. This well-defined trail leads to a ford across the stream. One last jog to the left (just below the stone wall) leads through mountain laurel to Burnham Brook. Follow the brook downstream (west) and across a feeder stream.

Burnham Brook is especially scenic here as it tumbles over broad, flat slabs of gneiss dating from the late Ordovician period, about 450 million years ago. The stream channel was carved by meltwater flowing from the glaciers. This old trough, which cuts down through the bedrock, used to carry a greater volume of water. It is now the site of the smaller, present-day Burnham Brook. Here you are at the edge of an extensive hemlock forest.

The trail leaves the brook and climbs diagonally up the southern bank with a view down on Burnham Brook. In April, this section of trail is carpeted with yellow, round-leaved violets. Continue, by way of a well-defined woods road leading uphill, to the corner of a five-foot-high stone wall marking the northwest boundary of the adjacent property, Dolbia Hill Farm. Once at the stone wall (note the huge stone pile at the corner), look for markers indicating a sharp turn to the right. This leg of the trail is a broad path that

*winds through hemlocks and mixed hardwoods to the
source of Nodding Fern Brook.*

Nodding Fern Brook rises in a wet pocket at the foot
of a rocky slope to the southeast of the trail, and flows
out of the Burnham Brook watershed. The rocks near
the brook support an interesting array of plant species,
from mosses and ferns to mountain laurel, dogwood, and
larger hardwoods. A sizable black birch, thrown over by
the wind, has ripped up the flat rock that once helped
anchor it, revealing its shallow root structure. Also note
that the high water table has filled the depression left by
the roots with water.

*The trail follows the stream for a short distance, then
turns left at a pair of markers, crosses Nodding Fern
Brook, and climbs diagonally to the right of a rock
slide. Watch your footing!*

The rock-slide is pretty well stabilized, as evidenced by
the vegetation. Lichens cling to the bare rock, while mosses
and the tiny fern, common polypody, occupy crevices in
the rock. Marginal wood ferns and white woodland asters
also occur amid the rocks. This is a cool north-facing
microhabitat. Herbaceous plants frequently tremble in the
slight breeze that rises through the narrow defile, hence the
name "Nodding Fern" Brook.

*At the top of the rise, squeeze through a narrow
opening between the ledge and a tree trunk and
follow the trail eastward along the crest of the ridge.
At the next pair of markers turn right and continue
across the abandoned Dolbia Hill Road Extension*

(note the old red cedar posts at the edge of the roadway). A short distance away, just in front of a large dead chestnut, go left to the top of the ledges and follow the trail northeastward for some distance.

The plateau above these ledges, which was grazed in the early part of this century, was an open-grown white oak stand twenty-five years ago. In the intervening years it was invaded by hemlock. In the summer of 1981, this entire ridge was defoliated by gypsy-moth larvae. The caterpillars' preferred food is oak leaves, but as they grow larger and exhaust their food supply they will move on to the heavier needles of the hemlocks. As you walk eastward along this trail, note the many hemlocks killed by this defoliation.

Gypsy-moth outbreaks are periodic. The last serious one on this land was in the mid-1960s. In the forest it is best not to spray, but rather to allow the infestation to run its course so that the moth population diminishes through natural controls. A study of the epidemiology of this insect was carried out on the preserve in the 1960s, because this was one of the few places where the population had not been disturbed by insecticides.

At one point on the southwest-facing slope there is a handsome beech stand. From this high vantage point you can look through the beeches, still coppery-green in early November, down the valley of the Eight-Mile River toward Hamburg Cove. Underfoot is a grassy herb, Pennsylvania sedge, and in June the rattlesnake weed (with yellow flowers and rosettes of purple-red veined leaves) is in bloom. The numerous uprooted oaks along the crest of the ledges were blown down in 1985 by Hurricane Gloria.

After about a quarter-mile the marked trail turns sharply right (southward) and drops from the top of

*the ledges on an old logging road. At the foot
of the pitch, turn left and follow the trail (no further
markers) northeastward to Dolbia Hill Road. The
entrance where you parked your car lies a short
distance along to your left.*

Below the ledges, keep an ear cocked for the dry buzz
of a worm-eating warbler along the wooded slopes. In
the more open woods, listen for the squeaky, running
notes of a blue-gray gnatcatcher and the buzzy song of
the cerulean warbler. Spicebush, with its pungent aroma,
occurs frequently in the moist soils below the ledges.
Look for its small yellow blossoms in early spring and
its red berries in late summer. These aromatic berries are
a favorite fruit of birds, rabbits, and deer. Be alert for the
blast-off of a ruffed grouse, and observe the enormous
glacial erratic to the left of the path. A glacier plucked
this huge boulder from the bedrock, perhaps miles away
to the northwest, and carried it in the southeast-bound
ice. Eventually, a warming climate stopped the glacier's
forward movement and, as the ice melted, the rock was
dumped on this slope. Beyond the erratic and to the right
(south) lies a red-maple swamp. The trail passes below the
Dolbia Hill house and then gradually rises to the paved
road.

The core of the preserve at Burnham Brook was donated
to the Conservancy by Richard and Esther Goodwin. Their
gift has been augmented by gifts from neighbors and by
purchases.

5

BUTTERMILK FALLS

Plymouth

*Walking—A small preserve that can be hiked in
about 15 minutes. Or take advantage of the Mattatuck
Trail and spend half a day hiking 3 miles to the Mad
River to see its cascades and pools in a hemlock gorge.
If you take a picnic, please remember to pack out your
garbage.*

---

*DIRECTIONS: From Bristol or Plymouth take
Route 6 to Terryville. Turn south on South Main
Street and follow it for about 2.8 miles to a
junction of several roads. Go left (east) on Lane Hill
Road. (Please note that this road is not plowed in
the winter.) The preserve lies 1,000 feet ahead on the
right-hand side of the road. Look for the blue blaze
of the Mattatuck Trail. If you plan to take the 3-
mile hike, park one car at the junction of Route 69
and Mad River Road in Walcott (just north of the
junction with Route 322).*

BUTTERMILK FALLS, tumbling over ledges in a series
of creamy-white cascades, is a favorite stopping place
for many Connecticut residents. The preserve features
an interesting steep-sided ridge, or kame, deposited as

a result of glacial activity. The soils along the watercourse are highly erodible sand and gravel known as terrace escarpments. They support hemlocks along the falls, and mixed hardwoods with an understory of thick mountain laurel on the moderate slopes to the south. The yellow of clintonia and the pink of lady's slipper brighten the forest floor.

It is disheartening to find this extraordinary natural area marred with litter. The town, in coordination with the local stewardship committee, has provided trash cans at two locations along Lane Hill Road, and the energetic preserve monitor rallies friends to make a springtime cleanup. Even so, this effort is scarcely adequate come summertime. The cool beauty of the preserve attracts party-goers like a magnet, and cans and bottles overflow the area.

Since this guidebook will never land in the offender's grip, it is for you, the enlightened reader, to lend a hand. The Conservancy angel will look kindly upon you if you will please carry out more than you carry in. Those who walk through Buttermilk Falls after you will enjoy it that much more.

If you choose to hike 3 miles, take the blue-blazed Mattatuck Trail across the bridge to the south.

The section of trail lying between Buttermilk Falls and Allentown Road is dominated by mixed hardwoods, oaks in particular. Mountain laurel is profuse. In fact, the entire length of the trail leading to Route 69 at Mad River Road features vast quantities of laurel. It is likely to be in full bloom by mid-June, making for a heady summer's walk.

Cross Allentown Road and go through the field directly opposite. Look for the blue blaze at the edge

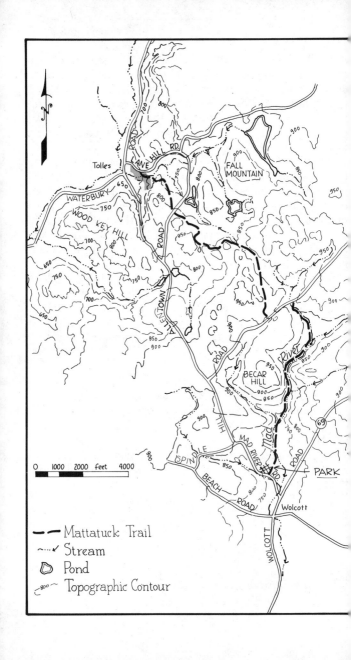

N

Tolles

LANE

HILL RD.

FALL
MOUNTAIN

WATERBURY

WOOD KEY HILL

ALLENTOWN ROAD

River

BECAR
HILL

MAD RIVER RD.

ROAD

SPINDLE

BEACH

ROAD

WOLCOTT

69

PARK

Wolcott

0   1000   2000 feet   4000

- - - Mattatuck Trail
~···~ Stream
⬠ Pond
~ 800 ~ Topographic Contour

*of the woods and follow the trail for just over a mile
to Spindle Hill Road.*

The trail, although wandering through very rough
terrain, climbs only fifty feet or so. Exposed outcrops
form sheer cliffs, and overhanging ledges are covered
in mosses and lichens. The soils are shallow to bedrock
and excessively drained. The oaks growing here appear
stunted, with some dead or dying. Only the mountain
laurel is vigorous. Toward the south, the open trail is
flanked by sheep laurel, a diminutive of the heath family.
Usually found in bogs and moist open areas, sheep laurel
appears out of place near the open trail. Look also for the
dark-green leaves of wintergreen growing flat against the
ground.

*The trail jogs left for a short distance on Spindle
Hill Road, then continues south in the woods about a
mile farther to Mad River Road at Peterson Memorial
Park, 0.2 mile north of the junction with Route 69.*

The first stretch of trail is along an old double-track
logging road, through an otherwise familiar oak-hickory
forest where the white birches appear very showy. The
road dwindles to a path filled with huckleberry. As the
slope steepens, the path becomes badly eroded and often
carries water following heavy rains.

The power-line cut provides an entirely different habitat for "weed" species that do well on disturbed sites.
Grasses and goldenrod have helped stabilize the open
ground. Look for the blue blazes that lead back into the
woods just above an old mill dam with stone foundations
at the edge of Mad River.

The Mattatuck Trail follows Mad River downstream past cascades and pools. One small footbridge crosses Break Hill Brook, which tumbles over rocks in a lovely hemlock ravine. The final hundred yards of trail leaves the hemlocks and enters mixed hardwoods where red cedar and yellow birch are very much in evidence.

Both the northern and southern ends of this hike lie in the depths of a hemlock gorge within sight and earshot of clear running water. Either location will provide a perfect picnic site, but please carry out what you carry in. There are trash receptacles at Peterson Memorial Park.

Buttermilk Falls Preserve was acquired using the Conservancy's revolving fund. Area residents subsequently raised funds to reimburse the Conservancy.

6

CATHEDRAL PINES

Cornwall

*Walking—Less than a mile through a strikingly
beautiful white pine stand, the oldest that Connecticut
(and perhaps New England) has to offer. The first
section of the trail rises steeply through the forest; the
rest is an easy romp, part of it on a paved country
road. A longer hike is possible by continuing in either
direction on the Mohawk Trail, part of the Connecticut
Blue Trail System.*

*DIRECTIONS: From the junction of Routes 4
and 125, go south into the village of Cornwall. The
road ends at Marvelwood School and faces Coltsfoot
Valley. Go left on Valley Road, which very soon
bears sharply right at the "Corner of the Pines." Take
the next left onto Essex Hill Road and continue for
0.2 mile. Park on the left at the preserve entrance sign
near the large boulder topped by a white pine.*

THE FORTY-TWO–ACRE CATHEDRAL PINES
came as a gift to the Conservancy in 1967 through the
generosity of three members of the Calhoun family: Jean
C. Bacon, and John and Frank Calhoun. The Calhouns
have long been the guardians of this tract, having bought

39

the property in 1883 to prevent its being logged. The stand is a mixture of mature white pines and hemlocks with some northern hardwoods.

*Follow the trail leading from the parking area
up behind the large boulder. It leads through a tangle
of elderberry and wild roses, past an uprooted white
pine, and connects immediately with the Mohawk
Trail. Follow the blue blazes in under the pines.*

Cathedral Pines has been recognized as a National Natural Landmark by the National Park Service. The area is the most massive single stand of old-growth white pines and hemlocks identified in New England and the Adirondacks. In 1988, the Connecticut Botanical Society presented The Nature Conservancy with a certificate of commendation celebrating the largest white pine tree in Connecticut, which is growing in Cathedral Pines.

Many have pondered the origins of Cathedral Pines, but there is no proven theory. Piecing together certain facts continues to be an intriguing process.

Unless influenced by some natural disaster, such as flood, fire, wind, or insect infestation, the natural development of an even-aged pine stand often runs as follows: an old field is abandoned and seeds in with white pine. In this northern climate of Connecticut, white pine, rather than red cedar, is a natural invading species, since it requires full sunlight to germinate and develop. As they grow, the young pines, mixed with a few hardwoods, crowd the field. With ensuing years, their branches collide and must compete for light. Many of the smaller trees are crowded out by the larger and healthier trees. As the forest canopy forms overhead, the lower branches of the pines are shaded and eventually wither and die. Because the trees grow close together with plenty of light from above, they develop straight, tall

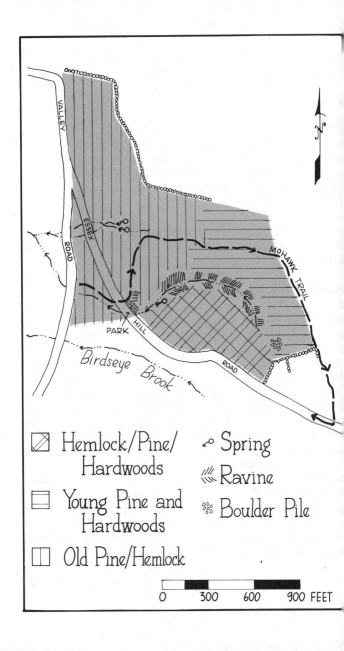

⊠ Hemlock/Pine/ Hardwoods	↶ Spring
▤ Young Pine and Hardwoods	⦚ Ravine
⊞ Old Pine/Hemlock	⸫ Boulder Pile

0	300	600	900 FEET

trunks. However, in the dense shade thrown by the mature trees, there is a distinct absence of white pine regeneration.

Another plausible scenario in white pine development occurs when only a few white pines invade a fully lit pasture. They have all the space they need to grow, and their lower branches develop and thrive in the full sunlight. Their open-grown form is quite distinct from the slender, towering giants of Cathedral Pines, and they provide a seed source for another generation of more closely spaced white pines.

Neither developmental sequence quite applies to the white pine and hemlock stand at Cathedral Pines. The dominant white pines here had been considered an even-aged stand, roughly two hundred years old, until trees blown down by a tornado in August, 1980, damaged a portion of the forest and provided The Nature Conservancy with an opportunity to take a much closer look at the stand. Each downed tree was methodically cored and accurately dated by counting annual growth rings. Unexpectedly, several three-hundred–year-old pines were discovered. Equally surprising, their diameters and straight-growth form were similar to those of trees a full hundred years younger that grew right next to them.

These discoveries posed new questions about the origins of the present stand. Had these older trees been part of an extensive white-pine stand which was lost to some naturally occurring disaster in 1780? Or had the two generations of pines been part of a northern hardwood forest whose hardwood component had been devastated by an insect infestation? It seems most unusual that so few three-hundred-year-old white pines remain, and that the ones the Conservancy found were so straight and slender.

The trail bends to the right and begins a steep ascent. At the top of the steep rise, the trail passes through more downed pines and hemlocks. These, as well as

*other trees to the right of the trail, were snapped
off or blown over by the 1980 tornado and merit
closer inspection. The taller stumps are full of beetles
and larvae, which are prey for woodpeckers. Observe
the large oblong cavities made by the pileated
woodpecker.*

Well to the north of the trail is the site of a specialized
logging operation. A contractor was looking for a stand of
long, slender white pines over a hundred feet in height, no
greater than eighteen inches in diameter at the butt, and
no less than nine inches at the tip. The white pines located
just to the north of what was to become the Conservancy's
boundary were found to be ideal for his purposes, and the
cutting began in 1953.

The contractor brought with him a team of Oneida Indians from upper New York State to do the cutting. The
trees were felled one on top of the other so that the tip of
the most recently dropped tree would cushion the fall of
the next tree brought down. In so gentle a fashion, a tiny
saw-whet owl was brought to earth unharmed.

The logs were piled onto a flat-bed trailer truck and
driven to New York. The stems were so long and flex-
ible that roughly two feet in length were lost as the tips
dragged and were shorn away during the drive. The logs
were ultimately used as pilings to support the Tappan Zee
Bridge across the Hudson River as well as Israel's Tel Aviv
airport.

*The trail swings south along the old logging road
and continues to Essex Hill Road. Turn west (right)
and follow this blacktopped road downhill back to
the boulder with the pine on top. In most seasons
you can hear nearby Birdseye Brook tumbling into
Coltsfoot Valley below.*

The growth of Cathedral Pines has been well documented over the past seventy years. Professor George E. Nichols, from the Yale School of Forestry, described and photographed the stand in 1913, and Henry Hicock, of the Connecticut Agricultural Experiment Station, wrote about Cathedral Pines again in 1956. A series of three permanent study plots was also established in 1956 by Herbert Cobleigh, then a forestry student at Yale. These same plots were remeasured in 1980. While the forest as a whole has looked much the same over the past twenty-five years, comparative data show subtle changes. Within this quarter century, several of the old pines and hemlocks have fallen over, allowing sunlight to reach the forest floor. These openings are filled with dense hemlock thickets. Hemlock tolerates shade but, once released, surges with growth in light. Other openings show increased growth in the herbaceous layer. Within this same period the canopy trees have increased their diameters by an average of four inches. Black birches, which were too slender to measure in 1956, have grown enough in diameter that they now occur in measurable sizes. Other than these subtle changes, and the obvious changes caused by the tornado, Cathedral Pines looks much as it did seventy years ago in Professor Nichols' photographs.

7

CHAPMAN POND

East Haddam

Canoeing, then walking—Between 3 and 5 miles, depending on which channel you use, along the Connecticut River, into the quiet waters behind Rich Island, and across the wide expanse of Chapman Pond. The steep hills of the eastern bank support hemlock and mixed hardwoods; low-lying, flood-plain forests and marsh land lie between the river and the pond. Plan your trip to coincide with high tide.

DIRECTIONS: Bring a canoe. From Route 9, take exit 7 to Route 82 and East Haddam. At the blinking light, jog left (north) on Route 154 and right onto Route 82. Once across the Connecticut River, turn right past the Gelston House and go south toward the Goodspeed landing strip. Park in the field between the paved parking lot for the Goodspeed Opera House and the landing strip, and launch the canoe from the sandy beach. (Canoes can be rented from Down River Canoes, across the river on Route 154, telephone 203-345-8355.)

Paddle downstream. Stay close to the eastern shore, keeping the main channel and both islands to your right.

CHAPMAN POND AND THE SURROUNDING area in East Haddam were the first lands between the English settlement at Hartford and the fort at Saybrook to be acquired by a white man. Robert Chapman of Saybrook purchased the land in 1642 from an Indian named Chapeto. At the time of the purchase, the pond didn't exist. In its place was an extensive meadow of salt hay that Chapman harvested seasonally, and which was known as "Chapman's Meadow." The property was eventually incorporated into the town of East Haddam, and a town highway was constructed at the meadow's edge. The old road survives as a footpath, and remenant bridge abutments are still visible. A portion of the meadow was converted into a town common for grazing.

Sometime before the mid-1800s the meadow washed away—probably the result of an extraordinarily high and violent flood—and the pond formed. It continues to be fed by the streams tumbling off the hills to the east and to be drained by two channels to the river. These channels serve as outlets during ebb and as inlets during flood. This direct connection with the Connecticut River creates a unique tide in the pond, and, unlike other tidal ponds that are saltwater or brackish, Chapman Pond is far enough upstream from Long Island Sound to remain entirely fresh.

At the southern end of Rich Island is one of the pond's two outlets (or inlets, depending on the tides). Either enter Chapman Pond here (especially if the wind is against you) or paddle another half-mile to the second channel, which is far more picturesque and winds northward into Chapman Pond.

The low-lying forest between the river and the pond is typical of the Connecticut River flood plain. The

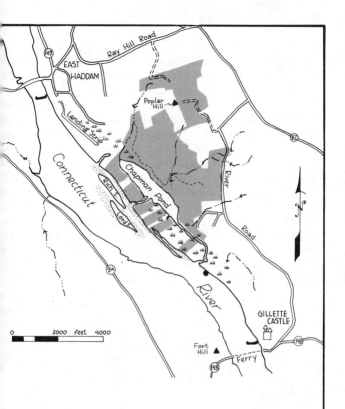

_{¹⁴⁹}

Ray Hill Road

EAST
HADDAM

Landing Strip

Poplar
Hill

82

Connecticut

Eight
Mile

Chapman Pond

River

River

Road

9A

River

GILLETTE
CASTLE

Fort
Hill

148

Ferry

148

0   2000 feet 4000

Stream
Wetland
Tidal Flat
Canoe Launch Area
Light
Trail

larger trees are red and silver maples, ashes, and cottonwoods. These species grow in a variety of soils and tolerate repeated periods of inundation, as do the shrub species—including alders, willows, and spice bush—found here. The herbaceous layer is the most interesting and botanically diverse. The open marsh land includes wild rice, pickerelweed, cattail, reed grass *(Phragmites)*, blue flag, yellow iris, and many species of sedge and rush. Of particular interest are two rare plant species that grow at Chapman Pond: Torrey's bulrush *(Scirpus torreyi)*, a northern species occurring on shores and in shallow waters; and a species of arrowhead *(Sagittaria montevidensis)*, another northern species.

Paddling north along the winding southern channel in the lee of the steep eastern shore, one is reminded of a slow-flowing bayou in a southern bottom-land. The water's edge is bright with color in the autumn—in particular with the brilliant red of cardinal flowers. Kingfishers keep pace with the canoe, bouncing up just ahead at each bend in the channel. They announce your arrival with an almost continuous rattle-like call. If you paddle quietly, you might flush a great blue or green-backed heron, or perhaps an egret; or you might spy an osprey perched on an oak's enormous bare branch spreading out over the marsh edge.

During the autumn migrations, ducks stop over in the quiet waters of Chapman Pond. One can expect to see hundreds of common mergansers, mallards, teal, black ducks, ring-necked ducks, and scaup. Canvasbacks, hooded and red-breasted mergansers, gadwalls, and widgeon are all present in lesser concentrations. The wetlands, in combination with the river and pond, is an excellent habitat for the river otter, mink, and muskrat. A word of caution during hunting season: duck blinds on adjacent private property are used occasionally.

Chapman Pond is home for over twenty-five species of fish, and a spawning site for alewives, an anadromous species that must spawn in fresh water and spend the rest of its life cycle in salt water.

The pond is equally important as a critical wintering site for many fish species resident in the lower river. The small volume of fresh water from feeder streams and the location of the tidal inlet along the western shore result in a large, undisturbed body of water with little current. This helps wintering fish to conserve energy, and consequently those in the pond are healthier than those that live in the river and must continually fight the current. Having protected Chapman Pond as a preserve, we can feel more confident about the long-term survival of these fish, since degradation of their habitat would seriously reduce their populations.

Paddle to the eastern shore directly opposite the more northerly outlet. Tie up securely and disembark to have a look at the upland. The former town road runs along the shore of Chapman Pond. Follow it for a short distance to the north and south to get a feel for the forest's cool depth and to observe the clear feeder streams. Please stay on the trail, which is dedicated to Lucy and Alexander Adams, two strong Connecticut conservationists.

The slope rises steeply for more than two hundred feet from the water's edge. A series of seven such rugged rock bluffs with sheer cliffs are separated from one another by streams that flow in alternating cascades and pools over slabs of bedrock. This series of hills is known as the Seven Sisters and extends along the river's eastern bank from East Haddam to Gillette Castle. The castle commands the view from the seventh sister overlooking the Hadlyme Ferry Crossing.

The vegetation of the uplands is largely mixed hardwoods and hemlocks, with more hemlocks on north-facing slopes and at the base of the deeper ravines cut by the tumbling streams. The mixed hardwoods develop best on the south-facing slopes. Here oaks, maples, beeches, and birches co-dominate, with tulip trees occurring on the wetter sites. A stand of mature tulip trees grows along the pond's eastern edge.

These wooded uplands provide an excellent habitat for most woodland wildlife species common to Connecticut. Deer and foxes reside in large numbers, and there is reportedly a healthy population of coyotes here as well. Once, in the hills above the pond, a naturalist heard a distinct yapping of coyotes, apparently triggered by the siren of the East Haddam swing bridge. Coyotes, however, are secretive species and are rarely sighted.

Paddle west across Chapman Pond and through the more northerly channel. Then turn upstream and paddle north a mile to East Haddam.

Three hundred acres of the core preserve were acquired by the Conservancy from the heirs of Vivian Kellems. This has been augmented by additional purchases, and by a gift of five and a half acres from Peter Paris. The preserve is named for Cynthia B. Carlson, a conservationist and long-time resident of the area.

DENNIS FARM PRESERVE

Pomfret

*Walking and ski touring—2 miles through old
agricultural land, most of which has now gone to oak
forest. The path is a well-defined farm road. The
route passes by a beaver pond on adjacent 4-H land
and returns by way of grassy (or snowy) Old Kings
Highway.*

---

*DIRECTIONS: From Route 44 at Abington, turn
north at the stoplight onto Route 97, and continue
north for 0.5 mile. Bear left onto Taft Pond Road,
and take the next left on Dennis Road. Proceed for
0.5 mile. Park at the head of Old Kings Highway
(just before reaching the farmhouse).*

*Leaving the car parked at the entrance to Old
Kings Highway, proceed on foot or by skis down
Old Kings Highway. Go left on a path that runs
beside the open field. Turn right down a farm lane
flanked by stone walls and fields.*

THE FIELDS ARE LEASED PERIODICALLY to
local farmers to mow or use for pasture. That way,
farmers gain use of the land, a precious commodity,
while the Conservancy maintains its open fields. It's an

arrangement whereby all benefit, including the bluebirds and tree swallows. Please be sure to close any gates you may open.

In the summer the massive trees growing along the stone walls shade the hiker. Most of these trees date back to the Civil War and before. Leaving the fields behind, the lane proceeds through a second- or third-growth oak forest. The soils along this broad hilltop are well drained. It is interesting to note that the fields used to extend over a much larger area, but since many were on poorly drained soils, only the few open fields that are on the best sites surrounding the farmhouse remain. Of the five homesites located on the Dennis Farm property, four were located on poorly drained soils and are now no more than empty cellar-holes.

The forest at Dennis Farm Preserve is quite homogeneous. The canopy is dominated by red and black oaks, with a shrub stratum of huckleberry and blueberry on the drier sites and mountain laurel or witch hazel on the richer slopes. The lower slope drainages support a red maple-yellow birch forest with an understory of spicebush.

The road forms a T near the southern corner of the preserve. Turn right (west) at the T and descend the hill to a gateway at the 4-H property.

The road swings around the headwaters of what was, until recently, an unnamed brook. Welcome to the diminutive watershed of Katherine's Brook, named in honor of the donor's sister, Katherine Dennis Smith. Growing close to the road are lady's slipper, pipsissewa, shinleaf, and rattlesnake plantain.

It seems that each preserve has its particular idiosyncratic feature; at Dennis Farm it is a strange-shaped tree

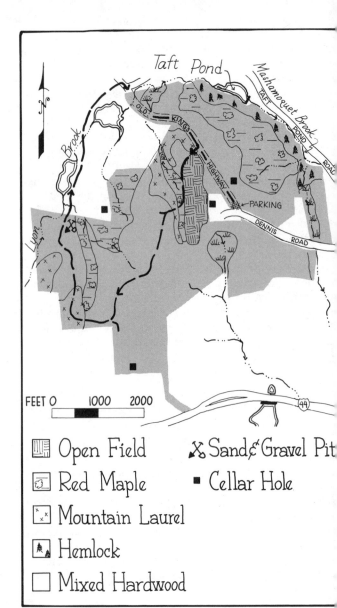

Taft Pond

Mashamoquet Brook

Brook

Lyon

OLD KINGS HIGHWAY

TAFT POND ROAD

PARKING

DENNIS ROAD

44

FEET 0   1000   2000

Open Field   Sand & Gravel Pit

Red Maple   Cellar Hole

Mountain Laurel

Hemlock

Mixed Hardwood

that just asks to be sat upon. Its horizontal bough was perhaps caused by another tree falling against it when it was
young, pinning it into this configuration. Watch for this
white oak on the right-hand side of the road.

*Go through the gate and onto 4-H property. Follow
the main camp road past a gravel pit, two ponds, and
out to the main road. Turn right, then right again
at a shagbark hickory and continue up Old Kings
Highway to your parked car.*

Lyon Brook flows through the 4-H Camp and into
Mashamoquet Brook out by the main road. Locals know
the former as Cudjo Brook, named for the last member
of the local Mashamoquet tribe. Whoever first mapped
the area for the USGS topographic quadrangle changed
the name to memorialize General Lyon, who was born in
Eastford (at the headwaters), and was the Union's first
casualty in the Civil War. The junction of Taft Pond Road
and Old Kings Highway is still known to old-timers as Cud's
corner (short for "Cudjo").

Beavers thrive in Cudjo Brook. Their lodge is situated
at the southern end of the first pond, and they wander far
up and down the stream. They are relative newcomers,
brought back to northeastern Connecticut some thirty
years ago. Game wardens from the New England states
brought natural-history exhibits to the 1954 Springfield
Fair. Following the fair, as the wardens from Maine were
packing up their stuffed moose and colony of live beavers,
the Connecticut warden proposed that he be allowed to
keep the beavers, at that time a species that had vanished
from Connecticut due to overzealous trappers. His wish
was granted, and he later released the beavers in this watershed. The colony increased, and individual beavers were
trapped for release elsewhere in the state. Today beavers

are quite common in both northeastern and northwestern Connecticut and coexist with a wide variety of wildlife. They are sometimes considered a pest requiring removal.

Great blue herons (whose rookery is five miles away) and green-backed herons frequent this first pond, as do occasional otters. A detailed study of the painted turtle population was undertaken at this pond, and turtles that were marked along the margins of their shells for the study still exist.

At the edge of the first pond, in the middle of the thicket of swamp azalea, sweet pepperbush, steeplebush, and meadow sweet, a pair of chestnut-sided warblers has taken up residence. At the crossing of Cudjo Brook look for joe-pye weed, cardinal flowers, and boneset.

The last leg of the hike follows Old Kings Highway, which led from Worcester to Norwich in the early 1700s. Today the stillness of the woods is broken only by an occasional pileated woodpecker. One local observer sees a direct correlation between white ash with heart rot and the presence of carpenter ants and pileated woodpeckers. Indeed, you can see the large oblong cavities made by the woodpeckers in ash trees on this north-facing slope. Listen for their distinctive call—a loud *kik-kik!*—and their drumming on dead wood.

Colonel Edward B. Dennis donated his farmland to the Conservancy in 1973.

DEVIL'S DEN

Weston

*Walking, ski touring—15 miles of well-maintained
trails cover this 1,583-acre preserve. The hiker can
enjoy a wide variety of terrain, from wetland, stream,
and pond, through mature forest to rocky knolls with
wide-open vistas. Devil's Den, whose many trails are
well marked with numbered posts, is worth exploring
on more than one visit.*

---

*DIRECTIONS: From the Merritt Parkway take exit
42 and go north on Route 57 for 5 miles. Go east
(right) on Godfrey Road for approximately 0.5 mile.
Turn left on Pent Road, which dead-ends at the main
parking area.*

DEVIL'S DEN IS AN ASSEMBLAGE of twenty-four
contiguous tracts acquired over the past twenty years.
Public use of the preserve is allowed from dawn till dusk.
Groups are required to obtain a permit prior to visiting
the preserve. Write Devil's Den, Box 1162, Weston, CT
06883, or call 203-226-4991.

*From the western side of the parking lot, follow
Pent Trail. Take the first left at post #3 on McDougal*

Trail (west). Bear left at post #16, then right at post #15.

This area was once cleared and farmed. To rid the fields of rock and keep livestock penned, old stone walls were built which now pattern the woods that have grown up over the past century. Clearing the fields must have been a momentous task, considering the vast amount of debris left by the glaciers some twelve thousand years ago. The terrain of Devil's Den is typical of much of southwestern Connecticut. High ridges of bare rock support little besides mosses and lichens. Valley slopes covered with a thin veneer of glacial till (accumulated soils and organic material) support mixed-hardwood forests and are drained by clear streams that have cut through to bedrock. Depressions, whether in the upland or lowland, hold moisture and support typical wetland vegetation, including red maples, and an understory of spicebush and sweet pepperbush. In spring the wetland crossed by McDougal Trail sparkles yellow with marsh marigolds. The forest of the midslope at Devil's Den is primarily oak, with white and red oaks dominant. The black birch, which can reach a relatively large twenty inches in diameter, became established at the time farms were abandoned, and is now an important component of these woods. White pines are almost totally absent, and hemlocks appear in small, poorly developed pockets throughout the natural area.

McDougal Trail, like many of the trails at Devil's Den, parallels the drainage between quite rugged topographic rises, about a hundred feet in elevation. As the trail passes to the south of many of these exposed knolls, notice the rough-edged cliffs "plucked" by the glaciers as they pressed down from the northwest and tore huge chunks off the southeastern edge of the exposed rock.

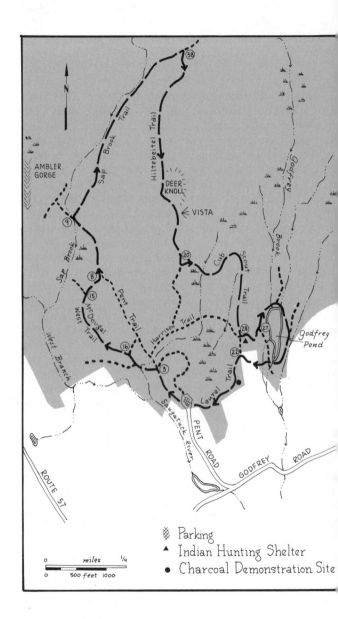

N

AMBLER
GORGE

Sap Brook Trail

Hiltebeitel Trail

38

DEER-
KNOLL

← VISTA

Godfrey Brook

9

Sap Brook

20

Cub Scout Trail

8

15

Pent Trail

McDougal West Trail

West Branch

Harrison Trail

16

3

28

27

Godfrey Pond

22

Laurel Trail

Saugatuck River

PENT ROAD

GODFREY ROAD

ROUTE 57

ROAD

❄ Parking
▲ Indian Hunting Shelter
● Charcoal Demonstration Site

0   miles   ¼
0   500 feet   1000

*At the top of a rise Pent Trail crosses McDougal
Trail. Bear to the left here at post #18 onto Pent
Trail. Continue for a short distance, and take the first
right on Sap Brook Trail at post #9.*

Sap Brook Trail climbs the western flank of an extended
ridge system running northeast–southwest. At the top of
the first steep rise, check for traces of large, milled timbers
at the sides of the trail. These poles and the anchor-holds
in the rock are all that remain from the old telephone
and telegraph lines and guy wires that used to connect
New York City and Boston. They might never have been
discovered were it not that an old American Telephone and
Telegraph right-of-way easement ran with the Devil's Den
deeds, indicating this past land-use. Even now, decades
after the original cut, it is possible to look north and
see that the larger trees stand about fifty feet apart, with
younger woods filling the gap where the telephone poles
and lines once ran.

*At post #38, turn right onto Hiltebeitel Trail and
proceed toward Deer Knoll.*

Hiltebeitel Trail travels through dense mountain laurel
which occupies much of the shrub stratum throughout the
preserve. In spring, look for the double-pointed deer tracks
in the moist soil, and be prepared for the sound of ruffed
grouse blasting off as you flush them from underfoot. Also
in spring, the vernal pools that fill the low-lying ground
are alive with the high-pitched jangle of peepers. White
azaleas grow in the depression situated in the saddle of
the adjoining ridges along Deer Knoll, and bloom toward
the end of May. From the highest point on Deer Knoll, it is

possible to see Long Island Sound on a clear day. Migrating hawks are also easy to observe from this vantage point.

The summit of Deer Knoll rises 485 feet above sea level and some 120 feet above its own base. The site's exposure influences the vegetation growing on it. Much light and wind coupled with little soil and moisture severely limit plant growth. Both the oaks and pitch pines appear tortured in shape and stunted. The massive bare rock, a resistant granite dating from the Middle Paleozoic, has been colonized by a variety of mosses and lichens. Soil which has accumulated in cracks in the rock supports little bluestem, huckleberry, and the low-bush blueberry. Just below the summit look for early blooms of lady's slipper, an orchid, warmed by the spring sun in a protected, south-facing site.

Follow Hiltebeitel Trail down the steep slope to the junction with Cub Scout Trail at post #20. Bear left on Cub Scout Trail till it joins Harrison Trail at post #28. Turn left again at post #27, and continue around Godfrey Pond.

At the junction of Hiltebeitel Trail and Cub Scout Trail there is a large mound of soil and rock debris partially covered by maidenhair fern. This pile is the site of a charcoal-tender's small cabin with a chimney at either end. When a section of woods had been cut over for charcoal and when the charcoaling was completed, the tender's cabin was deliberately razed. Some were easier to demolish than others. The Italian charcoal-burners' chimneys were beautifully laid and are still standing. The chimneys that the French-Canadian tenders built were haphazard affairs that collapsed readily when their huts were burned.

The trail passes right through a charcoal pit, the area where the charcoal smoldered. The soil remains blackened, and the hiker can observe small bits of charcoal mixed with the organic matter in the soil. Farther along, on Laurel Trail, is a charcoal demonstration site with a full-sized charcoal mound and a clear explanation of the entire charcoaling process.

Cub Scout Trail is named for its foster parents. Each year the local Cub Scout troop camps out at Devil's Den and, out of respect for the preserve, maintains this section of trail across log bridges and through mountain laurel.

Harrison Trail, leading to Godfrey Pond, passes a large Indian shelter created by a thirty-by-fifteen–foot rock overhang. The shelter was investigated in 1967–68, as were sixteen other sites in Devil's Den, and was found to be prehistoric in origin. Indians as far back as 5000 B.C. made periodic use of it for temporary shelter. Theirs was a seminomadic culture; small groups wandered through discrete territories hunting, fishing, and gathering. There is an informative display located at the side of the trail.

Turn left on Godfrey Pond Loop to circle the pond. Cross the dam over the outlet and continue straight at post #22 on Laurel Trail to reach the parking lot.

Godfrey Pond is surrounded by steep slopes supporting a mature mixed-hardwood forest. The pond's water level was raised by a thirty-foot–high dam of fieldstone and large stone slabs, probably quarried locally. At the southern end of the pond, adjacent to the dam, is the ruined foundation of a mill that dates from 1769. From 1797 to 1897 the mill was run by the Godfrey family. Following World War I, it passed to Yale University, then to the Bridgeport Hydraulic Company, and finally to the Conservancy.

The stone walls at this southeastern end of the preserve are remarkably high because they were erected to confine sheep. A narrow sheep-shearing run and some smaller enclosures, all built of stone, can be found south of Laurel Trail.

As indicated on the trail map available at the entrance, there are many miles of hiking trails at Devil's Den, and all are open dawn till dusk for public use. On the next outing, try a new trail.

The preserve's core, about 1,350 acres, was donated by Miss Katharine Ordway. Her extraordinary generosity and vision also led to the creation of much of the Conservancy's midwestern prairie system, encompassing tens of thousands of acres.

10

GRISWOLD POINT— GREAT ISLAND

Old Lyme

*Canoeing, then walking—1 to 2 miles along
a sand-spit extending into the Connecticut River. The
preserve provides an attractive beach with excellent
birding.* No pets, *please.*

---

*DIRECTIONS: Bring a canoe or motorboat. From
I-95, take exit 70. If traveling east, go south on Route
156 for 2 miles. If traveling west, go south on Lyme
Street and continue 1.5 miles through the village of
Old Lyme. Go left on Route 156 for 0.3 mile. From
Route 156, go right on Smith's Neck Road to the state
landing at the end of the road.*

*If you're not a canoe enthusiast and wish to walk
on Griswold Point, you may park at White Sands
Beach except from Memorial Day through Labor
Day, when it is restricted to Old Lyme town residents
with windshield stickers. From the parking lot, walk
below the high tide mark westward for half a mile to
Griswold Point.*

THANKS TO ITS UNIQUE LOCATION, Griswold
Point is one of the Conservancy's most prized natural

areas. No other major river in Connecticut is as unde-
veloped as is the vast network of salt-meadow marshes
and the sand-spit at the mouth of the Connecticut River.
To the west lie the cities of Stratford and Milford at the
mouth of the Housatonic River, and New Haven on the
Quinnipiac River; to the east lie New London and Groton
on the Thames River. In contrast, the broad Connecticut
River, longer than the Hudson and carrying a greater volume of water (it discharges 333 cubic meters per second
in an average month) separates the quaint village centers
of Old Saybrook and Old Lyme, whose combined population is only sixteen thousand. From a vantage point at
the westernmost tip of Griswold Point you can see a few
scattered residences to the north. Visible to the southwest
are the Old Saybrook lighthouse and, at a distance, the
low shoreline of Long Island. Standing here at the mouth
of this great river you can be quite alone.

*It doesn't matter in which direction you begin your
hike at Griswold Point. If you have come to watch
birds, you'll want the sun at your back as much
as possible. If sunbathing attracts you, spread your
towel. (Swimming is at your own risk.) Should you
wish to cross over the spit, please keep off the dunes
by following one of the two trails.*

The point is underlain by metamorphosed gneisses with
a mantle of glacial till laid on top. About thirteen thousand
years ago, following an extended period of severe cold,
the climate warmed, and the mile-high lobe of ice that
had extended south to what is now Long Island advanced
no farther. The meltwater pouring from the glacier's edge
dumped tons upon tons of rock debris along the ice margin.
This mountain of rock, called a terminal moraine, formed
Long Island.

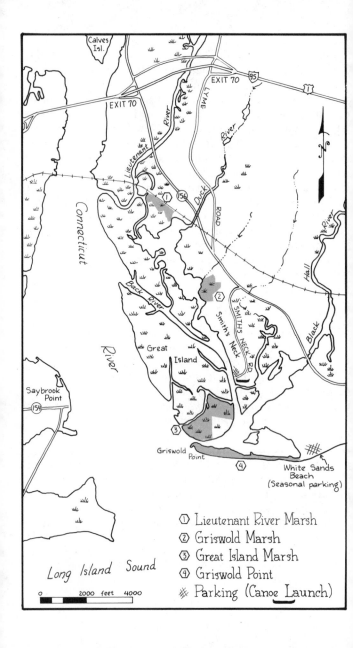

Calves Isl.

EXIT 70

95

EXIT 70

Lieutenant River

Lyme

Duck

River

Connecticut

156

1

ROAD

Back River

2

Great Island

Smith's Neck

SMITH'S NECK RD.

Hall River

Black

River

Saybrook Point

154

3

Griswold Point

4

White Sands Beach
(Seasonal parking)

Long Island Sound

0   2000 feet   4000

① Lieutenant River Marsh
② Griswold Marsh
③ Great Island Marsh
④ Griswold Point
✳ Parking (Canoe Launch)

As the climate continued to warm, the glacier receded and continued to dump all sizes of rocks and finer sands on top of the bedrock. This glacial material, called till, forms the core of Griswold Point's mile-long spit. The meltwaters caused the sea level to rise and so cut Long Island off from the mainland. The ocean currents moving from east to west through Long Island Sound are still reworking the configuration of the land masses. Griswold Point is still shifting, little by little, as these currents erode the eastern coastline, transport that sand and rock, and dump it along the western end of the point.

A local resident remembers the spit as being considerably shorter in length and lying further to the south, an observation confirmed in a 1917 U.S. Coast Guard chart. The point's northern migration is also evidenced by tongues of marsh peat extending from the south shore. These once-flourishing tidal marshes grew in the lee of the sand-spit's north shore and built up an organic peat-mat through the natural, seasonal decay of marsh plants. Then, as sand was deposited by sea currents, the marshes were buried. Now, decades later, these marsh peats are being unearthed by the same forces that caused them to disappear.

Across the channel and tucked behind the protecting arm of Griswold Point lies an intricate network of estuarine marshes—including Conservancy-owned Griswold Marsh and Lieutenant River Marsh—and portions of Great Island. These are all tidally regulated and extraordinarily valuable as spawning and nursery grounds for finned fish and shellfish.

The dominant vegetation is cord grass—both *Spartina patens* and the taller *S. alterniflora*, with their characteristic associate plants: black grass, sea lavender, and glasswort. Much of the marshland south of the Amtrak railroad-bridge is now protected by the State of Connecticut, the Old Lyme Conservation Trust, or The Nature Conservancy.

At low tide you'll be able to see the cobble-patterned bottom and the sandbars off the south shore of the point.

The sandbars are influenced by the longshore current, and migrate quite rapidly to the west. The changing morphology of Griswold Point has been mapped periodically by professors and students from the Department of Earth and Environmental Sciences at Wesleyan University.

Annual winter storms and periodic hurricanes cause major changes on Griswold Point. The Gale of 1815 washed away a portion of the bank to the east of the preserve, and with it a number of Pequot Indian graves. In 1954, Hurricane Carol ripped a breach through the point that later filled back in.

From a management point of view, the dynamics of nature mean that the Conservancy's plans remain fluid. If severely breached, the point might be entirely washed away, which, in turn, would destroy the extensive marsh system of the estuary. On the other hand, a storm that does slight damage may be propitious. In 1979, the sandy scar left by that winter's storm attracted a few pairs of least tern, at present on the state's list of species of special concern. Finding the bare stretch of high beach to its liking, this colony has returned to nest and has grown in number over the years.

The terns generally arrive in late May, when the days are growing longer and temperatures are moderate. The adults choose their nesting sites in slight depressions (scrapes) in the open sandy areas—sometimes perilously close to the high tide mark. Typically, a female will lay two eggs which hatch in late June or early July. The young terns resemble tan, speckled balls of fluff resting on the sand. They develop over the next month, learn to fly, and by the end of August migrate south.

When alarmed, the adult birds rise from their nests and dive-bomb the intruder, often aiming their droppings with remarkable accuracy! The birds' screams warn the young, well-camouflaged against the sand, to freeze for protection. If, by mistake, you have come with your dog, leash it and keep it well away from the nesting site. A dog running through the area can not only destroy eggs and young on contact, but can also rile the parent birds so that they fly off and remain away from their nests for too long. Unattended, the eggs or the young will soon die. After you have watched the terns for a little while, please be off and let them settle back on their nests. In an effort to protect this threatened species, The Nature Conservancy has erected seasonal fencing surrounding the least-tern colony. Please respect this barrier.

Piping plovers, on the federal endangered-species list, are also attracted to Griswold Point. An adult bird, about six inches long, is protectively colored and difficult to pick out against the sand until it runs. It feeds much like a robin, running a short distance then pausing with head cocked to one side, eyeballing a marine worm or small crustacean. Its nest is also a scrape in the sand where it usually lays four spotted eggs, almost invisible against the sand. Of the twenty or so pair that nest in Connecticut, generally two pair make their home at Griswold Point and will successfully fledge close to six young each year.

Griswold Point was for a long time a favorite spot for fishing and recreational camping—some families spent the entire summer on the point. The limit for camp sites was set at thirty for health reasons. Today, there is still some evidence of the tent-platform locations on the dunes, although the driftwood floors have been removed, and the beach vegetation is filling in the bare patches. The two cross-over paths were originally established by these seasonal inhabitants. Although it was Conservancy policy that finally brought the squatters' residency to an end in 1976, daytime use of Griswold Point is encouraged. During the summer months, a warden greets visitors, protects the least tern colony and piping plover nest sites, and keeps the beaches clean.

As you walk along the south side of the preserve, look for sea rocket with succulent leaves in amongst the driftwood on the upper beach. Its small purple flowers appear from July through September, and thereafter develop a distinctive double-seed pod. Even higher up the beach, at the dune's edge, look for the bright pink of beach pea, which, along with beach grass, admirably stabilizes drifting sand. Like most beach plants, these two have adapted to nutrient-poor, excessively drained, shifting soils. They gain nutrients and moisture largely from wind-borne saltwater spray.

Birders can look for nesting ospreys, which return at the end of March to court and to build their massive nests on the platforms to the north of the preserve and on Great Island. Sharp-tailed sparrows flit in and around the marsh on the northern margin of the spit. In winter, sea ducks and loons can be seen south of the spit, while buffleheads, goldeneyes, Franklin's gulls, and short-eared owls frequent the marsh.

Griswold Point was acquired through a series of bargain sales involving four donors, one of whom, Dr. Matthew Griswold, donated his interest in the land to the Conservancy. Mrs. Gertrude W. Barney gave the Lieutenant River Marsh. Griswold Marsh was a gift from Caroline Lane and W.E.S. Griswold. W.E.S. Griswold, Adela S. Bartholomew and Philip P. Johnston also gave land on Great Island to the Conservancy.

11

HIGBY MOUNTAIN

Middlefield/Middletown

Walking—A mile-long hike to the top of a basalt ridge that offers wide-open views to the south, west, and north over the Central Valley of Connecticut. The Mattabessett Trail follows the top rim along a sheer drop of 400 to 500 feet and, farther north, descends a talus slope. Not a hike for those who fear heights.

DIRECTIONS: It is possible to make the trip in one car, climb to the ridge, and return; or, park an extra car at the northern end of the trail, hike to it, and drive back. (Please note that Route 66 was renamed Interstate 691, just at the town line where Route 66 becomes a divided highway.)

To drop off an extra car: From Route 66 take Exit 13 near the Middlefield-Meriden town line. Follow the signs to the Police Academy on Preston Avenue. From the Police Academy driveway continue 0.6 mile north and turn right onto the dead-end road (before the underpass of Interstate 91). Follow the road to the end and park.

To trailhead: Park on the north side of Route 66 (heading west) just east of the Middlefield-Meriden town line at the brow of the hill where Route 66 becomes a divided highway. (From the parking area

*for the extra car, retrace the route along Preston
Avenue to the stop sign. Take a sharp left on East
Main Street and follow it east until it connects with
Route 66. U-turns are illegal, so at the next stoplight
turn around and head west on Route 66.)*

THE PRESERVE AT HIGBY MOUNTAIN protects a
representative sample of an important plant community
found on an exceptional geologic formation. Located
halfway between the coast and the northern uplands,
the dark trap-rock ridges that rise above the red-brown
sandstones are a unique habitat for specialized plant
communities. They also support certain plant species
that are of special interest because they reach the limit
of their range here. Species found on Higby Mountain,
such as yellow corydalis, are more common to the southern
Appalachians, while bearberry, also indigenous to this
ridge, is more typical of the summits of New Hampshire's
White Mountains.

*From the parking area, climb directly uphill on
a rough, stone-strewn path. Go left on a broad, level
trail, following the blue blazes of the Mattabessett
Trail. The trail makes a couple of switchbacks, dips
briefly westward, then climbs north along the ridge
edge to the highest point, the Pinnacle, 828 feet above
sea level.*

The talus slope inclining toward the parking area is
covered with a veneer of soils that is easily erodible.
Notice how the soil has washed from the rocks under
the foot trail. The hemlocks on this southeast-facing slope
have been almost completely stripped of needles by gypsy
moth caterpillars. In the next few seasons, especially if

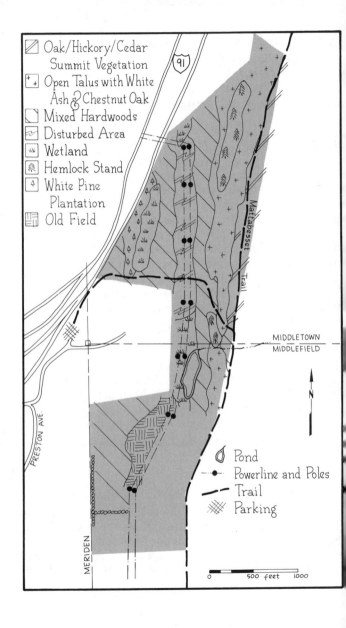

Oak/Hickory/Cedar Summit Vegetation

Open Talus with White Ash & Chestnut Oak

Mixed Hardwoods

Disturbed Area

Wetland

Hemlock Stand

White Pine Plantation

Old Field

91

Mattabesset Trail

MIDDLETOWN
MIDDLEFIELD

N

PRESTON AVE.

MERIDEN

Pond
Powerline and Poles
Trail
Parking

0   500 feet   1000

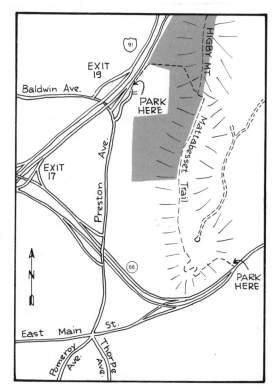

drought returns to Connecticut, we can expect to lose some hemlocks and hardwoods on Higby Mountain.

As you stop to pant on this steep ascent, notice how open the woods are. The poor soils support a sparse herb and shrub layer, and the bowed trunks of many of the mature trees show the influence of the unstable talus slope.

As the trail rises toward the summit, the vegetation begins to reflect the harsher microclimate. Given the dry conditions of these excessively drained soils, the upper talus supports only those species able to survive on very little moisture, such as chestnut oak and red cedar. The size of the oaks and cedars, as well as the hickories and other associated species, decreases as the elevation increases.

The canopy at the base of the mountain is at least fifty or sixty feet high, while at the summit it barely reaches six feet. The wind that blasts along the ridge stunts the trees. It batters woody plants, constantly prunes their outer twigs, and rapidly dries them out. The shrubs are also dwarfed by the harsh conditions and take on a bushy appearance, such as that of the viburnum that occurs on the cliff-side of the path at the summit. The herbaceous species are dominated by grasses that flatten in the wind and by other prostrate species with trailing branches, such as the bearberries that grow in the shallow pockets of soil on exposed rock.

Directly below the ridge is the shooting range for the Police Academy, generally not used on weekends. The major north-south highway is Interstate 91, connecting New Haven (south) and Hartford (north). On clear days the tall buildings of both cities are visible and, given the proper reflective lighting, Long Island Sound can be seen shimmering in the distance.

At the summit you are standing near the edge of a geologic fault on a ridge of resistant basalt dating from the Triassic Period some 200 million years ago. This volcanic formation is dark in color, being composed chiefly of silicates and oxides of iron. The rock is weathered in characteristic columnar blocks which break away from the cliff face to form steep talus slopes. The valley is underlain by more erodible Triassic sandstones. In these red beds a bulldozer operator first discovered the numerous dinosaur prints, located just to the north in Rocky Hill.

Either retrace your steps to the parking area on Route 66 or continue north along the Mattabessett Trail to Preston Notch. At the stream crossing, head downhill (although the main stem of the Mattabessett Trail continues north along the ridge).

Higby Mountain is part of a much larger system of north-trending basalt ridges that rise above the valley floor. To the west is Lamentation Mountain, over which the Mattabessett Trail passes. The Conservancy holds title to two other trap-rock formations: Bluff Head in North Guilford and Onion Mountain in Canton. While these fragments of basalt ridges are now protected, it is equally important that the continuity of these ridge systems also be preserved since they provide important corridors for some of the larger species of wildlife.

At Preston Notch, the hemlocks appear to be in good health—their location protects them from gypsy moths. Out of the wind, the trees grow taller, and the richer site also supports red oaks, white and chestnut oaks, and sugar maples, red maples, and shadbushes. Wildflowers are especially abundant here.

Leave the blue blazes of Mattabessett (ridge) Trail and follow the old road down diagonally across the talus slope and into the southwest corner of Middletown. Go gently over the loose rock. Continue directly across the power line right-of-way toward Interstate 91. On the elevated road bank, turn left (south) and continue a short distance to the parked car at the dead end of Old Preston Avenue.

The angular rocks that have broken away from the cliff face, known collectively as talus, form a steep slope. It is a dynamic site supporting poorly developed vegetation. The rocks continue to shift downslope, and so the plants that grow in the pockets of nutrient-poor soil are constantly uprooted. Many larger trees on the talus have developed a bow in their trunks because the weight of the rock continually shoves them downslope. Poison ivy is well developed here and covers wide expanses of bare rock.

During the summer of 1981, a Conservancy student-intern, who was preparing a natural resources inventory of Higby Mountain, was startled by a large white furry beast darting over the talus. It was a domestic goat turned wild that locals have occasionally glimpsed over the past few years. These rocky slopes are also home to the black racer snake, which has the frightening habit of vibrating its tail in dry leaves to simulate a timber rattlesnake! There are, however, no real rattlesnakes on Higby Mountain.

The power line right-of-way that follows the base of the cliffs is unsightly, yet it increases the diversity of vegetation within the Conservancy's preserve. "Weed" species became established in the mineral soils exposed when the line was strung. Goldenrods, roses, sumac, dogwoods, grapevines, and red cedars are all typical of old-field succession.

Well to the south of the trail leading west is an interesting wetland. Situated at the foot of the talus slope, and visible from the ridge, this wetland has been partially dammed by the power-line maintenance road and now forms a shallow pond abounding with turtles, water snakes, frogs, and various bird species.

The forest that lies between the power-line cut and Interstate 91 is typical of the area. A third- or fourth-growth mixed-hardwood forest occurs on the flat valley floor. Many of the trees have multiple stems—proof that they developed as stump sprouts following the last lumbering operation. Farther west and off to the right is a small plantation of white pine. The fields to the left are private property and should be respected. The trail follows the perimeter of this property and leads to the parking area.

About 122 acres of the Higby Mountain Preserve were donated to the Conservancy by Howard and Frances Houston in 1979, with another thirty-seven acres given by an anonymous donor in 1986.

12

IRON MOUNTAIN

Kent

Walking—1.5 miles along a blazed trail, through an abandoned apple orchard, across a charcoal pit, and over the summit of Ore Hill.

DIRECTIONS: From the junction of Routes 7 and 341 in Kent, take Route 341 east for 3 miles to South Road. From the junction of Routes 45 and 341 in Warren, take Route 341 west for 4.2 miles to South Road. Take South Road 0.6 mile and turn east (left) on Treasure Hill Road for 0.5 mile. The parking lot and entrance sign are on the west (right) side of the road.

IRON MOUNTAIN, one of many hills situated to the east of the Housatonic River above the village of Kent, supports a second- or third-growth forest dating from the last extensive logging done in the nineteenth century to fuel the iron furnaces. Iron Mountain was named for one of the area's better-known iron mines, which is located off the preserve. There is an overwhelmingly beautiful view of the countryside from the western end of Flat Rock Road, a short distance from the preserve entrance and well worth the detour.

Follow the trail leading from the north of the parking area. It leads downhill to the west for some length, then turns south, following the slope contour, to an abandoned orchard.

The west-facing slope is characteristic of much of the woodland at the 283-acre Iron Mountain Reservation. Typical of northern hardwood forests, the preserve's well-drained uplands are dominated by large sugar maple, ash, red oak, and black birch trees. Prior to the early 1900s, the American chestnut was also a dominant species. The understory is largely filled with young hardwoods, maple-leaved viburnum, and witch hazel. The forest floor supports the grassy-looking Pennsylvania sedge and the sweet-smelling, hay-scented fern, as well as clubmosses and partridgeberry.

The many stone walls that pattern the woodland date from early colonization and the clearing of the land. Because they are so steep, cleared areas probably were grazed, rather than cultivated.

The stream, which in summer can only be heard but can be seen once the leaves have fallen, flows over private property beyond the preserve's northern boundary, which should be respected. This is one of two streams that feed Irving Pond below (also privately owned).

On the steepest incline of the trail there is a large, thirty-inch–thick American chestnut stump dating from approximately 1910, when the chestnut blight swept through the chestnut's natural range, killing the species. The wood was prized for its size, strength, and great beauty, and its loss caused a major impact on the forest industry. Much of the diseased wood was salvaged from the forests and stored for future use. Caches of chestnut lumber, milled in the early 1900s and hidden in barns, are still being discovered.

The lower slopes of the west-facing hill are quite moist, even in summer. In early spring, different types of violets

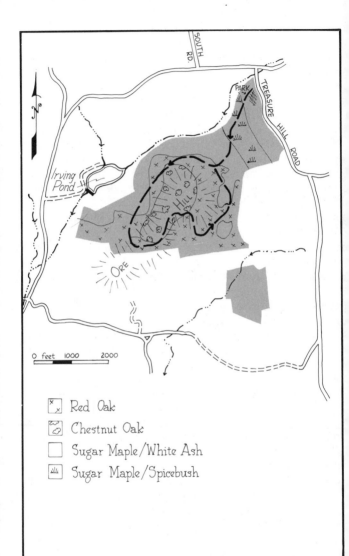

SOUTH RD.

PARK

TREASURE HILL ROAD

Irving Pond

HILL

ORE

N

0 feet	1000	2000

☒ Red Oak

☒ Chestnut Oak

☐ Sugar Maple/White Ash

☒ Sugar Maple/Spicebush

carpet the slightly elevated terrain at the edge of the
wetland. The two large trees that appear like sentinels
at either side of the trail are shagbark hickories. The
ground beneath them is strewn with the thick husks that
cover the hickory nutshell. Nearby are a number of large
hophornbeams, a tree that ordinarily reaches only three
to four inches in diameter. More typical of poorly drained
soils are yellow birches with spicebushes underneath.

Crossing an old woods road, characteristic of the many
overgrown roads forming a network across Iron Mountain
Reservation, the trail soon drops past two huge, open-
grown sugar maples. Their broad-reaching branches are
now bare, and the trees appear to be dying. They are
probably well over two hundred years old.

There is a long traverse across the base of the hill where
the poorly drained soils remain soggy even in summer. It
is a curious site on which to find an old apple orchard, but
here it is, caught up in a tangle of grapevines. Intermixed
with the fruit trees are spicebushes and an herb layer of
sensitive ferns and skunk cabbage. The orchard extends
onto moderately well drained soils where large, double-
stemmed black birches now grow between the rows of
apple trees. The ground is covered by lush Pennsylvania
sedge.

*The trail exits the orchard through a stone wall, turns
west (right), and meets the loop-trail junction. Turn
north (right again) and pass back through the stone
wall. Follow this trail, which becomes an old road,
for approximately 0.3 mile, to a junction on the
south (left) of the road.*

The far western end of the orchard is slightly higher,
with well-drained soils that support shagbark hickory.

There are probably two dozen large hickories growing
here to the exclusion of most other species. The trail soon
picks up an old level road that runs around the shoulder
of Iron Mountain. On the north-facing slope, the forest
composition changes to include other hardwood species
such as large, white paper birches which lend a distinct
northwoods flavor, and black cherry and beech trees. There
are also numerous black birches and occasional hemlocks

A large yellow birch on the left of the trail stands opposite an enormous boulder, or glacial erratic, measuring
twenty by thirty feet across and ten feet high. The erratic
was dumped off a retreating glacier as it melted some fifteen thousand years ago. Now it is draped in grapevines
and a few cherry saplings have taken root on top.

*It's fairly easy to miss the trail looping to the
south (left). If you come to a spring that issues from
several boulders on the south and privately owned
Irving Pond that lies just ahead, you have gone too
far. Retrace your path approximately 300 feet and
take the trail, now on your right.*

The hike uphill goes through a remarkable stand of
striped maple, so named for its green-and-white-striped
trunks. This species has enormous leaves (sometimes eight
inches across), which some say resemble the webbed foot
of a goose. In full summer, the greenish light that filters
through these great flat leaves is especially pretty. Violet
and Canada mayflowers cover the trail in early spring
and shadbushes blossom in the increased light at the trail
edge. As spring progresses other plants flower, including
starflowers, wild geraniums, and wild sarsaparillas.

This side of the mountain is peppered with charcoal
pits left from the mounds of smoldering hardwood burned

to produce charcoal. The level, circular areas, measuring twelve to fifteen feet across, still have small chunks of charcoal just below the surface of the ground, and the soil is charred a rich black. There is one pit directly in the trail's path.

As the trail rises, the forest composition changes. The large hemlocks that occupy the midslopes are stunted at higher elevations, and at the summit they are totally bare of needles—victims of gypsy-moth caterpillars. The summit is dominated by multiple American chestnut sprouts intermixed with chestnut oaks. These, too, have been attacked by caterpillars. Only huckleberry and low blueberry continue to thrive, along with an occasional mountain laurel.

The summit is also characterized by handsome outcrops of gray-to-pink gneiss, with darker black mica (biotite) present in quantities from flecks to streaks. There are also small amounts of magnetite—naturally magnetic lodestone, an important ore of iron—on the reservation. (If you have a compass with you it may behave erratically, thanks to an abandoned magnetite mine which lies outside the reservation.)

The descent from the summit is quite steep, and passes great slabs of bedrock with common polypody ferns growing on them. Here the hemlock has fared better and still retains its needles. Farther below, the trail runs through old fields that are now reverting to young woods. Blackberry and raspberry bushes are quite frequent, and in other places Pennsylvania sedge carpets the forest floor.

At the junction with the loop trail, go straight through the stone wall (bearing right) and follow the same trail by which you entered and continue across the abandoned apple orchard, through the forest, and out to your car.

The 257 acres of the reservation were donated to the Conservancy by Mrs. Walter E. Irving in 1974, with subsequent gifts totaling twenty-six acres given by Brigitta Lieberson and Joseph Gitterman.

13

LORD COVE

Lyme

*Canoeing—5 miles of paddling (best at high tide).
Lord Cove, with its maze of waterways, provides new
discoveries with each twist in the channel. There is also
excellent birding.*

---

*DIRECTIONS: From 1-95, take exit 70 and go north
on Route 156 for half a mile. The town landing lies
off to the left; you may launch the canoe there, but
you may not park. The nearest legal parking is at the
park-and-ride lot just north of I-95, about half a mile
from the town landing.*

THE TOWN LANDING LIES OPPOSITE Calves Is-
and, off the main stem of the Connecticut River and a good
two miles south of the Conservancy's preserve at Lord
Cove. Both Calves and Goose Island are entirely com-
prised of marsh land which, since Long Island Sound is
only two miles away, is influenced by the daily tides.
Recently, silt and sand dredged from the river's channel
have been dumped on the islands, covering over the
native salt-meadow grasses (*Spartina*). The result is a
"disturbed" substrate on which reed grass (*Phragmites*)
typically proliferates to the exclusion of the native species.

Paddle northward, keeping close to the eastern bank of the Connecticut River and leaving the islands on your left. The steep hill on your right is Quarry Hill. Once in the open waters of Lord Cove, keep to the channel marked by buoys. A maze of waterways lies to the north. There is no given route; explore the channels on your own. It's impossible to get truly lost, but you do get quite turned around! It's also best to pay attention to the tides to avoid sandbars in the upper end of Lord Cove that may trap the canoe at low tide.

The vast expanse of water is deceptively shallow and at low tide provides excellent feeding areas for herons and egrets. Farther north, where the channel narrows, the eastern shore rises abruptly, and the excessively drained soils support an oak-dominated forest (red, scarlet, black, and chestnut oaks) with shadbush and mountain laurel in the understory.

The narrow, winding channels of Lord Creek and Deep Creek to the north allow a quiet canoeist to approach many types of wildlife at each turning. Kingfishers and green-backed herons keep pace with the canoe by darting just ahead. Turkey vultures and red-tailed hawks, as well as ospreys and an occasional bald eagle, soar overhead. A kestrel may hover on high as a lone marsh hawk glides over the marsh. Occasionally, a great blue heron lifts off from the water and, with labored, slow-motion wing beats, makes its slow progress farther upstream. In the autumn, ducks abound, although they are wary and skittish because hunting is allowed on the adjacent state-owned land (a good reason to avoid visiting the area during waterfowl season).

Fortunately, the duck hunting is seasonal and only temporarily disturbs an otherwise remote and tranquil estuarine marsh. Equal in size to the extensive tidal marshes

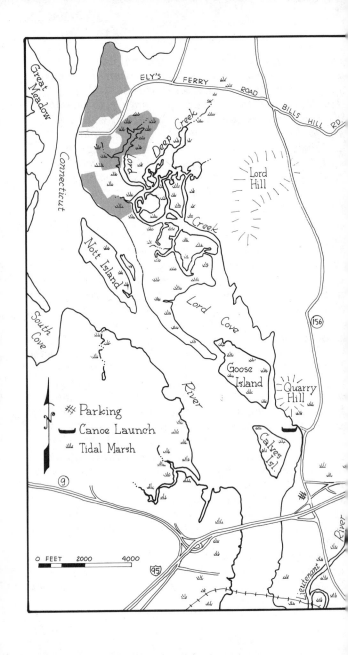

of Great Island and its environs, tucked behind Griswold Point to the south, the Lord Cove marsh complex is far better protected both from storms blowing off the Sound and from boat traffic. It is an important habitat for many species and has tremendous potential for biological production of invertebrates, fish, shellfish, birds, and mammals.

Lord Cove has fewer man-made ditches than the areas to the immediate south, which favors the growth of indigenous vegetation and has enhanced the marsh's ability to trap silt and pollutants carried down by the river. The cove, with its numerous "holes" and channels, is remarkable for its pure beauty, as well as for its value in mitigating floods and recharging ground water. It is also a welcome aesthetic respite from an increasingly built-up environment.

There is good variety in the vegetation communities within the preserve. Most of them are influenced by their proximity to the brackish tidal flushings that occur twice daily. The water decreases in salinity upstream, to the point that it becomes entirely fresh at the head of Lord Creek and Deep Creek. Consequently, the vegetation has become characteristic of a freshwater marsh, dominated by two species of cattails. These flower in early summer, and the male inflorescence, or blossom, is covered with a heavy yellow pollen—reportedly a fine substitute for baking flour. Closely associated with the cattail marsh, and dependent upon it for food, cover, and shelter, is the muskrat. It not only feeds on the starchy white rootstocks and new shoots of the cattails, but also uses the cattails to build its lodges. The lodges, which are visible from a canoe, are connected to the creek margins by tunnels.

The marsh boasts many bright-colored flowers: yellow iris at the channel edges in early June, followed by yellow bur-marigolds and the pink of swamp rose mallow later in the season. The tall grasses of wild rice and prairie cordgrass along the channels provide food for waterfowl during the fall migration and the winter months.

Red maple swamps lie at the northern reaches of both creeks. These swamps are important links between the upland and the tidal marsh because they help regulate water distribution in the estuary. During times of flood these areas absorb excess water, slowly releasing it during periods of drought, thereby helping to maintain a constant long-term moisture level.

The uplands lying between Deep Creek, Lord Creek (not part of the preserve), and the steep slopes and rock outcrops to the north of Ely's Ferry Road are the remnants of the coastline of the postglacial period. These rocky slopes hold very little moisture for plant growth and support mostly oaks and hickories, with huckleberries beneath, on the most exposed sites. The soils of the lower slopes tend to be deeper and richer in nutrients and can therefore support beeches and hemlocks.

To the west of Lord Creek, the cattail marsh gives way to agricultural land that is still mowed annually. Deer are a common sight here, and the open meadows attract the bobolink, a songbird easily recognized by its black breast and white rump. This grassland is plagued with two bothersome alien plant species. Indigo bush and reed grass reproduce vegetatively by root suckers and runners, and are taking over growing space from the native grasses. Comparing old photographs with more recent ones illustrates clearly the widening colonies of reed grass.

Beyond this open meadow stands a flood-plain forest characteristic of the Connecticut River Valley. The moderately drained alluvial soils support species that tolerate periodic flooding, such as black cherry, black locust, and black gum trees along the Connecticut River bank. This community is also subject to occasional wind and ice damage.

The uplands of the preserve to the north of Ely's Ferry Road have a very shallow soil layer above the bedrock. The excessively drained and extremely rocky Hollis soils do not retain moisture and are prone to drought. Given these conditions, fire threatens this fragile area (there have been two in the recent past) and public access is limited. Access to upland areas is allowed only with advance permission from the Connecticut Chapter of The Nature Conservancy.

Donors of land for the preserve at Lord Cove include Richard and Stanley Cooper, Chamberlain Ferry, and Leontine Harrower.

14

MEADOW WOODS

Essex

Walking—2 miles through extensive oak-hickory woodlands that were once open farmland. A side trail leads through rich woods to a spring. The terrain is varied, while the vegetation is remarkably homogeneous.

DIRECTIONS: Take Route 9 from Middletown or Old Saybrook to the Essex exit (exit 3). Follow signs for Essex along West Avenue. Turn left on Grove Street at the library and continue to North Main Street. Go left again and continue on North Main for 0.6 mile. (North Main Street becomes River Road.) Turn left on Book Hill Road and continue for 0.7 mile. Turn left on Book Hill Woods Road and park at the end of the cul-de-sac. Here you'll see a blue nature-preserve sign for Canfield Woods (adjoining Meadow Woods Natural Area) and a brown map box.

The trail leads into the woods via an old right-of-way bridging a drainage basin. Climb over the rough ground and bear to the left. Trail 3—the perimeter trail—leads you just over 2 miles through Canfield Woods to the Conservancy's Meadow Woods Natural Area. There are also two shorter

hikes: Trail 1 offers a mile-long loop and trail 2 closer to 1.5 miles.

MOST OF THIS 323-ACRE NATURAL AREA was once cleared for agriculture, and the woods are still laced with handsome stone walls. The broad, fairly level expanse of Book Hill was most likely abandoned at one time, as indicated by the fact that the red cedar that invaded those fields are now topped by even-aged mixed hardwoods. Notice the rusty barbed wire imbedded in these cedars as you walk south along the trail.

Shortly after trail 2 peels off to the left, you'll notice chestnut sprouts that appear quite healthy, and farther on you'll pass through a stone wall. It is possible to take a half-mile side trip to the spring at this point by following a tan-colored "Spring Trail" sign located on your right at the stone wall. Follow the tan arrows northwest over a slight rise and continue downhill toward the spring.

The stone walls that parallel the trail leading to the spring follow the ridge summits. This major ridgeline runs north–south and is flanked by gentler slopes to either side. It was originally laid down as sediments in the Cambrian Period, some six million years ago, then metamorphosed into crystalline gneisses. The gneisses, in turn, were invaded by igneous intrusions of granite and basalt.

The series of glaciers that followed many thousands of years later alternately scoured the landscape as they moved southward, and then deposited a mantle of glacial debris as climates warmed and the glaciers receded. The terrain at

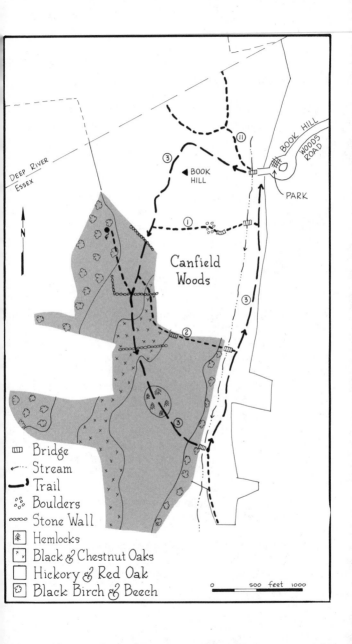

DEEP RIVER
ESSEX

BOOK HILL

Canfield Woods

BOOK HILL
WOODS ROAD
PARK

N

① ② ③ ⑪

Bridge
Stream
Trail
Boulders
Stone Wall
Hemlocks
Black & Chestnut Oaks
Hickory & Red Oak
Black Birch & Beech

0   500 feet   1000

Meadow Woods is typical of this glacial activity. Its summits are bare rock outcrops; its gentler slopes and valleys are filled with glacial till.

The spring is located midslope in a slight depression. Water-bearing rock strata reach the surface here, allowing water to seep out and flow as surface runoff. The added moisture is reflected in the surrounding plant growth. A large tulip tree grows just to the east of the spring.

Retrace your steps uphill and notice some of the largest trees in the preserve—black and white oaks, with chestnut oaks along the excessively drained ridge. Once you reach the stone wall, regain the blue trail 3.

Stone walls that once kept the cows from the corn now keep the cut-over woods from a forest allowed to grow. The oak woods to the south of the stone wall were known as the "Williams Property." They have not been logged for over a century, and large, scattered, open-grown oaks stand tall. The younger forest to the north of the stone wall is dominated by black birches and beech saplings. Even the larger white oaks are double-stemmed, indicating past logging and regeneration by stump sprouts.

The midslopes of Meadow Woods, covering at least half of the preserve, are dominated by red and white oaks, pignut and shagbark hickories, black birches, and less frequently by beech trees. The dominant shrub is maple-leaved viburnum, easily distinguished by its downy leaves shaped like red maple leaves. In spring, these slopes boast a wide array of wild flowers, including bluets, bloodroot, and early yellow violets.

The path descends through a patch of hemlock, one of a very few areas on the preserve in which this species occurs. Before gypsy-moth caterpillars recently damaged the two mature hemlocks, they produced enough cones to establish their own "brood" of seedlings, now standing ten to fifteen feet tall. Hemlock was excluded from the drier sites of these woodlands, most likely due to recurring fires to which it is especially sensitive.

The southeast-facing slope has the characteristically rocky substrate of well-drained Hollis and Charlton soils. It appears to have been overgrazed or clear-cut, which accelerated the soil erosion along the steeper slopes. Observe the manner in which many trees, their upper roots exposed, are straddling the rocks to either side of the trail.

The trail proceeds downhill and crosses the unnamed brook that runs along the eastern side of the Natural Area. Once across the brook, turn left (north) and follow the trail the full length of the preserve. Jog right toward the end of the trail to return to your car.

Earl and Margaret Canfield donated ninety-seven acres to the Conservancy to create Meadow Woods. In later years, they sold 226 acres known as Canfield Woods to the towns of Essex and Deep River. All told, 323 acres are now permanently protected.

15

MILO LIGHT NATURE PRESERVE

Montville

Walking—2 miles along old logging roads through mixed hardwoods typical of eastern Connecticut. The trail runs past an old foundation, with a pretty prospect across Trading Cove Brook, and returns along a power line right-of-way and a loop trail back through laurel and hardwoods.

DIRECTIONS: Milo Light lies between Salem and Norwich, just north of Route 82. From Route 82 take Route 163 north for 0.3 mile. Go right on Hershler Road (road sign frequently missing) and continue 0.2 mile. The entrance, marked with a yellow Nature Conservancy sign, is on the right between Kingdom Hall of the Jehovah's Witnesses and a small house. There is space for one or two cars on the right-of-way. Follow Trail 1 eastward to the power line right-of-way. (Don't be lured onto Trail 2, 3, or 4.)

THE TOPOGRAPHIC RELIEF of Milo Light Nature Preserve ranges 120 feet, with swamps filling the depressions and bedrock outcrops of gneiss capping the ridges and forming steep ledges. While the terrain appears rough

and the vegetation impenetrable in places, the old road is well laid and the walking is easy. The uplands are almost entirely mixed hardwoods dominated by oaks and hickories. Prior to 1910, the American chestnut was also an important component of this forest. Its rot-resistant stumps occur throughout the preserve, and some produce sprouts two or three inches in diameter. The American chestnut was attacked by a virulent strain of fungus that decimated the population in 1910. Many of the trees were salvaged for their valuable timber, creating openings in the canopy which, in time, were filled primarily by oaks.

The understory and shrub stratum are filled with diverse species. The drier uplands support huckleberry and mountain laurel while the richer midslopes are filled with dogwood and azalea which flower in May. Witch hazel and maple-leaved viburnum also abound. The wetter sites are dense with thick stands of sweet pepperbush which flower in June and fill the woods with a heavy, sweet scent.

This main trail follows the old road through woods that were cleared in colonial times and past a former farm. Stone walls that bounded the fields are still very evident. Some fields, abandoned relatively recently, still support the first trees that seeded into them, such as red cedars, although these are mostly dead or dying. Clubmoss, a genus that indicates past clearing and grazing, covers wide expanses of the forest floor here.

Once past Trail 4 that branches downhill to the brook, watch for foundation walls to the north (left) of the path. These and other foundations on the rise of land between the road and the brook have been traced to Daniel Appley, who homesteaded at this scenic location around 1870. When the leaves have fallen, there is an especially nice view down the hill and over a small dam that crosses Trading Cove Brook.

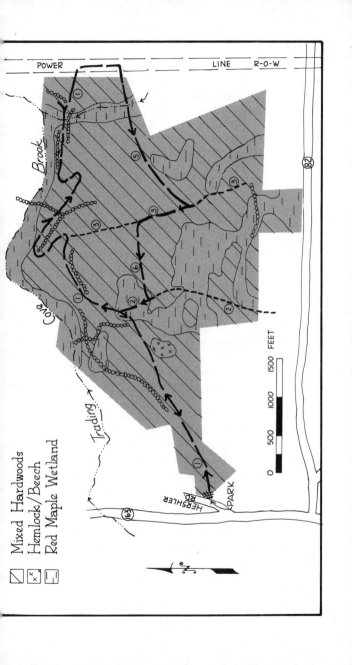

Mixed Hardwoods

Hemlock/Beech

Red Maple Wetland

POWER   LINE   R-O-W

Brook

Cove

Trading

PARK

HERSHLER RD.

POWER LINE R-O-W

28

163

0   500   1000   1500 FEET

N

Turn south (right) and follow the maintenance road under the power lines for a quarter mile. Count the pylons and, as you pass the third one, turn right and walk diagonally downhill toward the wetland. (You may have to bushwhack a bit.) At the base of the hill, walk directly toward the woods and you will see the yellow NATURE PRESERVE sign.

The power-line right-of-way borders the Conservancy's eastern boundary and, while not a part of the nature preserve, it allows easy access to a southern trail leading back through the preserve. The right-of-way also increases the diversity of wildlife you are likely to see. Cutting for the right-of-way disturbed the soils and the vegetation they supported. As the soils settled with time, an entirely different kind of plant community—one that tolerates mineral soils, open sunlight, drier conditions, and variable temperatures—developed. Among this new community are blackberries and raspberries, thick tangles of poison ivy, grapevines, Virginia creeper, and mats of hay-scented fern. The taller, woody species appear stunted, having been sprayed with herbicides years ago.

Birds abound. Listen for the high-pitched, screeching call of red-tailed hawks which frequently perch on the power-line towers, and look for red-breasted grosbeaks and prairie warblers. From the woods on either side you can also hear ovenbirds and veeries, among other species.

Follow Trail 5 into the woods (now Conservancy-owned land) and continue to the junction with another woods road. Turn north (right) on Trail 3, left on Trail 6, right on Trial 2, and left on Trail 1, to return to the car.

In summer, it's a relief to come away from the baking sun and return to the cool shade of the forest, and in winter, the forest protects the hiker from the cold blasts that are funneled along the power-line cut. This forest path leading westward into the preserve disappears among the mountain laurel and is especially enjoyable in June when the laurel is in full bloom. During the growing season, there is also an array of wild flowers. In May, the edges of the paths suddenly turn purple, blue, pink, and white with bluets, violets, wild geraniums, and lady's slipper.

William and Anne Alquist donated 338 acres to the Conservancy for this preserve.

16

POQUETANUCK COVE

Ledyard

Walking or canoeing—A 1.5-mile walk on a gentle footpath through post-agricultural land now grown to mixed hardwoods, and out along a steep promontory that juts into Poquetanuck Cove. Or canoe on the quiet waters of Poquetanuck Cove and paddle under the steep hemlock bluff. If by canoe, plan your trip to coincide with high tide, as the cove becomes a mud flat by low tide. There's good birding whichever way you go.

DIRECTIONS: From Interstate 95, go north on the Connecticut Turnpike (I-395) to exit 79A and take Route 2A east. Cross the Thames River and keep on Route 2A as it jogs north (left) with Route 12, then east (right). Proceed on 2A for 1.4 miles to the center of Poquetanuck. Go right on Cider Mill Road (which turns into Avery Hill Road). The preserve entrance is well marked on the right in 0.9 mile.

IF YOU HAVE BROUGHT along a canoe, you will want to take your first right off Avery Hill Road on Arrowhead Drive. Go to the end and turn right on Royal Oaks Road. There is a paved boat launch into Poquetanuck Cove at

the cul-de-sac. Park to one side, well out of the way of others.

If you are walking, from the parking lot at the preserve entrance, head west along the well-defined trail. It will make one stream-crossing, pass through a stone wall, continue along a broad hilltop, then drop into a hemlock forest at the edge of Poquetanuck Cove.

In May, the woods are alive with birds. First to greet you may be an ovenbird—the loud volume of whose call is remarkable coming from such a small (six-inch) member of the warbler family. Listen for its repeated chant in rising crescendo: "teacher, *teacher,* TEACHER!" The ovenbird is commmon to Connecticut's woodlands, though its domed nest—built on the ground and made of leaves and mosses—is well camouflaged and difficult to locate.

Later in the season the mating and nesting activity abates as the warmth and humidity increase, and the birds are silent at midday. Then, by late August, the drone of the insects takes over, and the rasping call of the katydids is almost constant.

If you have set out in spring or summer, a variety of green plants carpets the forest floor. At the edge of the parking lot you'll see such familiar species as false Solomon's seal with its rather showy plume of creamy-white flowers. In early spring, when plenty of sunlight reaches the forest floor, the oval leaves of Canada mayflower emerge. There is also an abundance of clubmosses throughout the preserve—a plant that typically establishes itself following field abandonment.

Overhead is a mixture of hardwoods common to this part of Connecticut. Oaks, hickories, beech, birches, and

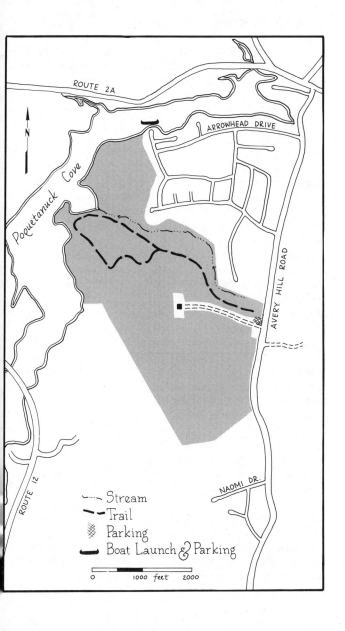

ROUTE 2A

ARROWHEAD DRIVE

Poquetanuck Cove

AVERY HILL ROAD

ROUTE 12

NAOMI DR.

- - - Stream
- - - Trail
※ Parking
— Boat Launch & Parking

0   1000 feet   2000

maples form the forest canopy in the eastern half of the preserve. The understory is a variety of species that thrive in
filtered light and include ironwood, viburnums, and blueberries. These trees and shrubs form a relatively rich woods
fed by nutrients and moisture moving downhill with each
rainfall.

If you are skeptical of the theory that water, nutrients, and soil move in quantity down slopes, take a
look at any of the stone walls that follow the contour
of Poquetanuck's terrain. The level of soil on the downhill side of the stone wall will have dropped several inches
as compared to the level of soil on the uphill side, where
the wall invariably blocks the movement of soil down-
wards.

Before crossing the intermittent stream, look for a handsome, pasture-grown, white oak. At one time its branches
had all the room to spread wide for sunlight, but now they
are hemmed in by younger trees. This lone "wolf tree"
most likely served as a rubbing post and shade tree for
hot, fly-ridden cows.

As you cross the stream, do you notice a slight variation
in temperature and humidity? Often a seemingly insignifi-
cant change in elevation, such as the drop of one or two
feet to cross this stream, is sufficient to cause a trough
along which cooler and moister air flows. Proof of this
microclimate is the cloud of mosquitoes you may encoun-
ter here. While the water appears clear, especially during
spring flow, it is not safe to drink. The added moisture in
the ground supports typical wetland species, including the
rank-smelling skunk cabbage and the false hellebore with
ribbed leaves. A variety of ferns also lives in this moist
habitat.

Hay-scented fern, characteristic of better-drained sites
where the forest canopy has opened to allow sunlight to
strike the ground, grows over an extensive area a little farther along the trail. If the day is warm, you can probably
catch the tell-tale aroma of the plant.

Once across the stone wall, you'll find the broad hilltop levels off and the dead or dying red cedar of the old fields are overtopped by black birch and hickories. The herb layer boasts a healthy growth of poison ivy, so keep strictly on the cleared path. On the far slope of the hill you'll discover a small, man-made open field. The uneven ground is the result of past archaeologists who dug in an Indian midden, or refuse heap. Look closely and you'll still find pieces of white oyster-shells which were discarded following successful oyster-digging in Poquetanuck Cove.

The hemlock forest occurs on the north-facing slope and almost takes the hiker by surprise. At one moment you are in full sunlight, the next you are in deep shadow. Lower your voice, feel the cooler air, and concentrate your senses. There's an inner excitement and anticipation. If you move slowly and keep your eyes fixed on Poquetanuck Cove, chances are good that you'll spot something. Black ducks and cormorants are common, and you may even startle an osprey or great blue heron. The mud flat and brackish tidal marshes of the cove are significant because horned pondweed, a rare plant in Connecticut, is found in these waters.

The trail through the hemlocks is narrow, and the slope steep with few hand-holds. Take care! Follow the trail out from the dark into the light deciduous forest. Continue downhill, along the level stone wall, then proceed diagonally uphill to reconnect with the inbound trail. Turn right and head out to the car over now-familiar territory.

As the cool north slope becomes more westerly-facing and the hillside is exposed to the buffeting winds from the southwest, the hemlock component of the forest is replaced by pitch pine and mountain laurel.

If you are walking in May, keep a lookout for the pink of a lady's slipper, an orchid, along the stone wall. Also look for evidence of the former giant of the deciduous forest, the American chestnut. Its durable wood is still intact in a seventy-five–year old stump.

The bright red berries of the sprawling partridgeberry on the west-facing slope provide food for ruffed grouse, so keep your ears open for low tom-tom–like beats that speed up to a whir and abruptly stop. You have just heard the drumming of a ruffed grouse, a sound made by the rapid beating of its cupped wings to signal the male bird's territory or to call to a female bird.

This lovely 234-acre tract was generously given by Desire Parker to The Nature Conservancy in 1988. When Miss Parker bought the property from a farmer in 1948, she promised never to develop the land. True to her word, she has provided lasting protection for the land and its creatures.

17

ROCK SPRING

Scotland

*Walking and (on wider paths only) ski touring—A
3-mile loop, with two options for shorter hikes,
leading through mature oak forest, open fields, and
along the clear-flowing Little River. The trail follows
woods roads and paths over an open esker and
through a dark pine plantation. A side trail leads to an
exceptional view of Little River Valley.*

---

*DIRECTIONS: From Willimantic follow Route 6
east. Turn right on Route 14 and continue east
through Windham and Scotland. Take Route 97
(Pudding Hill Road) north toward Hampton. The
preserve is east of Route 97 (right-hand side), 1.5
miles from the junction with Route 14. Roadside
parking is available for approximately six cars.*

THE 445 ACRES of this preserve are typical of Little
River Valley. The ridgetop supports oaks, and the acreage
below leads downslope through mixed hardwoods to
the undulating valley floor. Underlain by gravel and
sand, the valley holds a few kettleholes, which fill
with water during the wet seasons. Near the river
are a series of eskers—winding ridges formed by

glaciers—supporting very scanty vegetation due to excessively drained soils and lack of nutrients. Indian Spring, at the southern end of the preserve, is the first destination.

From the parking area, take the white-blazed trail leading directly east past the entrance sign. The perimeter trail, which this guide describes, is blazed in white. Shortcuts back to the parking area are blazed in white and red from the esker and in white and blue from Little River. The side trail to the lookout is blazed in white and yellow.

The entire east-facing slope of this wildlife refuge was at one time cleared for agriculture. The outline of the fields, marked by stone walls, is especially visible from late fall to early spring when there are no leaves. The oak and hickory trees of this forest are well spaced and straight, and appear to be the same age. The most common shrub in these extremely stony, sandy loams is maple-leaved viburnum. Both spotted wintergreen and the more intricately patterned rattlesnake plantain lie to either side of the trail. About a thousand feet from the preserve entrance and just uphill from the first stone wall, to be crossed perpendicularly, lies an extensive patch of round-leaved violets, an uncommon species in the refuge. Look for their yellow blooms in early May. Skeletons of red cedars, early old-field invaders long since dead, scatter this midslope site.

Where the trail intersects a white-and-red-blazed trail a sign indicates the direction both to the esker

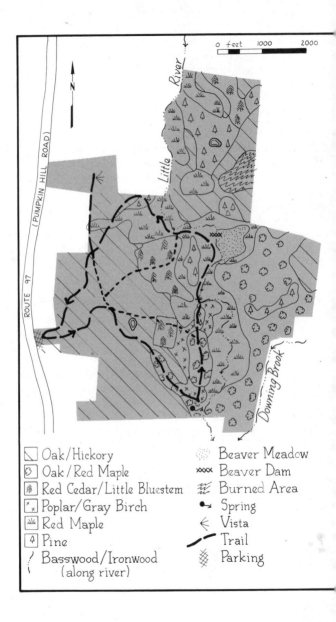

☐	Oak/Hickory	⬚	Beaver Meadow
🄾	Oak/Red Maple	✕✕✕	Beaver Dam
🌲	Red Cedar/Little Bluestem	≋	Burned Area
✕✕	Poplar/Gray Birch	•⤳	Spring
🌿	Red Maple	⬅	Vista
🄿	Pine	▬ ▬	Trail
⸝	Basswood/Ironwood (along river)	※	Parking

0 feet 1000 2000

N

(PUMPKIN HILL ROAD)

ROUTE 97

Little River

Downing Brook

and to the spring. Follow the white blazes to Indian Spring.

The white-blazed trail follows a broad road which the preserve committee maintains for emergency access.

To the east (left) of the road lies a vernal pond, almost a quarter-acre in area. It originated as a kettlehole about twelve thousand years ago following the final retreat of the Wisconsin glacier. A block of ice "stagnated," once broken from the glacier, and melted at this site, forming a round, steep-sided pond that has since considerably filled in with vegetation. During wet seasons the groundwater level of the entire valley rises several inches, which is sufficient to fill this depression. Frogs lay their eggs in this water in the spring; but, as the summer progresses, the water recedes until the groundwater level falls below the surface of the kettlehole floor, and the area dries up. Only those tadpoles hatching from the eggs laid earlier have sufficient time in the water to mature into frogs; the others perish.

The path leads out of the forest into an old field. Be alert for wildlife. Most of the saplings and shrubs you pass show signs of browsing deer. Notice also the variety and abundance of clubmosses, including several circular patches of *Lycopodium obscurum* on the southwestern (right) side of the trail. It appears that once established, the plant grows in widening concentric circles. The outermost margin is relatively well developed and lush green even in winter, while the inner circle of growth appears yellowed and weak, a direct result of the sandy soils, depleted of nutrients by the older clubmoss.

Indian Spring is now hidden by a stone structure, erected on a gravel bed in an effort to keep the water pure. Just downstream from it, you can still observe spring bubbling from the sand. The entire flow of this stream erupts in this fashion from underneath the stone covering. The water is cold, even in the middle of summer.

Retrace your steps for a short distance and continue directly north up the slope of the esker. Just over the brow of the hill a trail sign indicates the white-and-red–blazed shortcut that leads back to the parking area. The white-blazed trail leads to the right into a pine plantation and along Little River.

The esker is a remarkable geologic feature. It was formed in much the same way that a sculptor fills a plaster cast. As the glacial ice melted, rivulets of water formed under the ice sheet, sculpting elongated caves in the ice. These hollow channels later filled with sand and gravel debris to form what is known as an esker.

The soils overlying the esker are excessively drained with very little organic material. The trees tend to be dwarfed and only those plants that can tolerate poor soils become established. Here, yew, bayberry, reindeer lichen, and lone pitch pine help stabilize the erodible soil. The hiker may see both the brilliant red of British soldier lichen and the tiny green goblets of pixie cup lichen.

At the foot of the esker lies a small pine plantation, now roughly fifty years old. The trees grow close together and allow very little light to reach the forest floor. There is virtually no herbaceous growth, just a cushiony mat of pine needles. Most of the trees are red pines, whose lower branches drop off neatly once shaded out. At the north end of the stand are a few white pines with dead lower branches still intact. The temperature under the pines is noticeably cooler than in the surrounding fields and forest and, for this reason, the stand attracts wildlife. Owls frequent the area, as their pellets—fur-clad balls full tiny rodent-bones—testify. Raccoons are regularly seen hiding high in the bushy crowns of the pines.

At the northern end of the pines, the trail turns west (left) and crosses a small tributary via a bridge built by local Boy Scouts. Follow the trail upstream (north) along the west bank of Little River. Be forewarned that beavers periodically cause flooding of parts of the trail.

During the winters of 1981–82 and 1987, beavers, who have lived here at least thirty-five years, began to tackle the large oaks that line the river banks. You can't miss these oaks; most are twenty-four to thirty inches in diameter with neatly girdled trunks. One local outdoorsman believes this activity to mean that the beavers are depleting their preferred foods, willow and poplar, and have reluctantly turned to oak to keep their teeth a manageable size. (Beavers need to chew to wear down their teeth, which continue to grow.) By killing the oaks, they open the canopy and create conditions favorable to shade-intolerant, fast-growing species, such as the palatable poplar. Beaver mud slides punctuate the river bank.

While the beavers manipulate the environment to an important degree and cause flooding behind their dams, they also help maintain an open vista of the river for human visitors.

The trail, hugging the river, climbs a hill and turns abruptly south at a lofty, forty-foot–high lookout. Follow the switchbacks downhill and continue several hundred feet to a junction in the trail. The white-and-blue trail leads off to the left (south), providing a

shortcut back to the parking area. Straight ahead, the
white-blazed perimeter trail runs across a log bridge,
along the river, and eventually up a gradual rise
through woods.

The trail skirts a field in which sizable red cedars grow.
They have a distinctive shape tailored by hungry deer
which browse the lower limbs as high as they can reach
with outstretched necks. The path leads through thick low
blueberry and sheep-laurel. The river meanders in tight
S-curves and is periodically jammed with fallen logs and
debris. These temporary dams cause flooding and litter
the trail with flotsam.

As the trail bends away from Little River, it traverses
a mixed-hardwood and white pine forest. Look for twin
white pines grown together via a horizontal branch. Soon
after the twin white pines, the softwoods drop from sight,
and at the stone wall you'll see an entirely different type of
forest where the sugar maple is an important component
of the oak-hickory association. There is also a noticeable
lack of shrubs.

The last section of trail passes through an oak forest
and along stone walls, and leads out to the parking
area.
A white-and-yellow–blazed side trail leads off
to the north (right) to a massive stone bench facing
an awesome view of Little River Valley and eastern
Connecticut. Retrace your steps to the white-blazed
trail and hike uphill to the parking area.

On some days, the view is endless. In early spring before
the leaves have unfurled you can look across all of eastern
Connecticut. The pale hues of the hardwood forest give

way to the darker green of hemlocks in the valleys, and white pines are silhouetted against the horizon. On a still, warm day, you can hear Little River from the valley below, and several hawks might soar overhead, balanced on thermal currents. A garter snake might slither underfoot, almost invisible in the leaves. The view is calming and renews the spirit.

David and Vanda Shoemaker donated land for this preserve to the Conservancy. It was later augmented by a purchase from a neighbor.

18

SELDEN CREEK

Lyme

*Canoeing—A 4-mile trip, best done at high tide,
but navigable by canoe even at low tide. Keep to the
narrow creek, or circumnavigate Selden Neck, which
rises more than 200 feet above the Connecticut River.*

---

*DIRECTIONS: The boat launch lies within Gillette
Castle State Park immediately north of the Chester-
Hadlyme Ferry dock on the Lyme (east) side of
the Connecticut River. There's plenty of room to park
your car and easy access to the river's edge. Canoes
are available for rent here.*

FIRST, A WORD OF CAUTION: The substantial tides
in the lower Connecticut River (about 4 feet), combined
with the river's swift current, the wind, and the powerful
backwash of the ferry as it docks, makes navigating
difficult. Proceed with caution, and time your trip for
fair weather and helpful tides.

*Point your canoe downriver, negotiate the ferry, then
keep to the eastern bank. The first inlet, marked by*

a red tower labeled "A," leads to Whalebone Cove (more later in this chapter). The next inlet, opposite a green marker buoy numbered "37," is the entrance to Selden Cove and Selden Creek. The cove is shallow, so keep to the northern shore of the island. Turn right (south) and paddle a good mile to the southern extreme of Selden Neck.

Selden Neck gets its name from an early landowner, Selden, and reflects the past climatic history of the area. Once connected to the mainland via marshes, the neck was severed by exceptionally high water (possibly a storm in the mid-1850s) and the island—some 520 acres in size—was created. These waterways, tucked out of sight behind the massive hill that forms the island, have long been known to provide shelter for mariners. The wind that can sweep along the main channel of the river never reaches the narrow creek.

The State maintains Selden Neck as a State Park where only canoeists may stay overnight (one night only) for a nominal sum. There are forty-six campsites grouped in four areas, each with a fireplace and an outhouse. The park is open from May 1 through September 30, and reservations should be made at least two weeks in advance by asking in person or writing the park manager at Gillette Castle State Park, River Road, East Haddam, CT 06423. Reservations will not be taken by telephone, although you may wish to call about campsite availablity (203-526-2336). The island is worth a stop. Discover its old quarries, whose granite was shipped (along with brownstone from Portland, to the north) to New York.

The lower elevations at the northern end of Selden Neck reflect the past clearing of this area, now grown to red cedar trees and grasses. There is a landing here with rustic steps leading away from the water and over the alluvial soils deposited with each flooding of the river. The higher

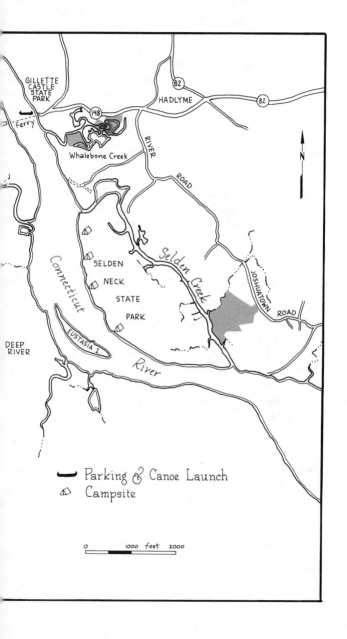

GILLETTE
CASTLE
STATE
PARK

Ferry

148

HADLYME

82

82

Whalebone Creek

RIVER

ROAD

Selden Creek

SELDEN

NECK

STATE

PARK

Connecticut

JOSHUATOWN ROAD

DEEP
RIVER

EUSTASIA I.

River

N

⊏ Parking & Canoe Launch

◿ Campsite

0   1000 feet   2000

elevations typically support oak-hickory forests with hemlocks on the steep slopes and ravines.

During the warmer seasons, when the steam train makes its run between Essex and Haddam, you can hear the distinctive wail of its whistle as it reaches Deep River and Chester. It brings back the past when the river was used much more for commerce. Imagine wooden-hulled ships steaming along the channel instead of today's loud, gas-guzzling speed boats.

Selden Creek is a popular thoroughfare, though its shallow, narrow course often pressed against sheer cliffs dictates that boaters proceed gently and with respect. As you paddle southward, the creek grows yet narrower and is flanked by rich marshlands. Look for soaring marsh hawks and ospreys. Ospreys are also frequently sighted perched in branches overhanging the creek feeding on a recent fish catch. If you should surprise this large bird with its catch, note how it flies clutching the fish, head forward, in its massive talons.

Savor the beauty of the granite cliffs covered in hemlock and the cooler temperatures they cause. The cliffs and the rope swings that dangle beside them are a magnet to the adventurous. On a hot summer's day, there is likely to be too much commotion for wildlife to linger nearby. However, on a quiet day there are duck, kingfisher, river otter, and a variety of fish to be observed and enjoyed.

At the base of one cliff on the eastern side, you may spot an old brass boat-ring set permanently into the rock. Also, look in nearby rock crannies, just above the high tide mark, and you may discover the deep blue of bottle gentians or the bright red of cardinal flowers.

A natural levee has built up along the southern end of Selden Creek and is held in place by the root systems of typical floodplain tree species, in particular the dominant silver maple. Beyond the levee are the tidal wetlands extending inland to the base of Observatory Hill and Shippy Hill. Between the two hills, The Nature Conservancy holds title to fifty-five acres. Another forty-six acres are protected by conservation easement through the generosity of Ferdinand Coudert.

On reaching the Connecticut River, please take into account the tide, current, wind, and boat traffic before judging whether to return via the Connecticut River or Selden Creek. Once returned to the red tower labeled "A," you may wish to dart in to see Whalebone Cove.

Whalebone Cove boasts a rich abundance of wildlife resulting from the unique qualities of tidally regulated freshwater. There are extensive mud flats for waterbirds to rest and feed on as well as one of the largest stands of wild rice along the river. A rare species in Connecticut, golden club (*Orontium aquaticum*), is also present in Whalebone Cove.

Twenty-five acres of this important ecosystem were donated by Mrs. Philip Schwartz.

19

SPIDERWEED

Middletown

Walking—3 miles through dry oak woods, along massive rock outcrops, over a rock bluff with a view, down to a stream, past overgrown fields, and along an old farm lane.

DIRECTIONS: From Middletown or Old Saybrook take Route 9 to exit 10. Follow the ramp to the stoplight, turn left (north) on Route 154 (Old Saybrook Road), and continue for 0.7 mile. Just beyond Paul's Auto Body, take a right onto Dripps Road (gravel). The road immediately bends to the right at a junction with the preserve's entrance at an old grassy lane. Park at the side of this little-used town road. Follow the white blazes up the old road.

THE ROAD RISES through an oak-hickory forest which was heavily defoliated by gypsy-moth caterpillars during the summer of 1981. This infestation weakened trees already growing under stress on poor sites. Here stony, excessively drained soils are shallow to bedrock and hold little moisture, so as the road climbs the hill, there are progressively more dead hardwoods. The white pines

have not fared very well, either. The younger trees on the right-hand side of the road are completely denuded and dead, while the mature pines higher upslope on the left barely hold their own.

The road turns and follows the edge of an unnamed stream where the microclimate is damper. Sugar maples, ashes, black birches, and yellow birches comprise the forest canopy. There is a small pool built into the streambed, and the area is rich with salamanders. The roadbed here is lush with moss during wetter seasons.

The stone walls that pattern the woods on the route uphill date from early colonial days, when many of the gentler slopes were used for pasturing sheep and cattle. However, throughout the 1800s manufacturing industries began to flourish along the Connecticut River, and the cleared land on the hills was left to revert to woodland.

At the top of the climb, the road levels out and leads east. Follow it approximately 200 feet and look for a yellow-blazed spur trail leading to the overlook on the right.

The lookout is formed by a huge pegmatite intrusion. This rock, approximately 300 million years old, intruded into the older (500-million-year-old) host gneiss. The pegmatite, more resistant to erosion, has remained, while the other rock has weathered away. Notice the characteristically large feldspar and quartz crystals. Feldspar has been mined for its valuable beryl content from similar rock located north and just west of the preserve. Beryl is a very strong, lightweight mineral used in the aerospace industry.

This exposed rock is a typical site for pitch pine. (See chapters 2 and 11 for descriptions of similar terrain and

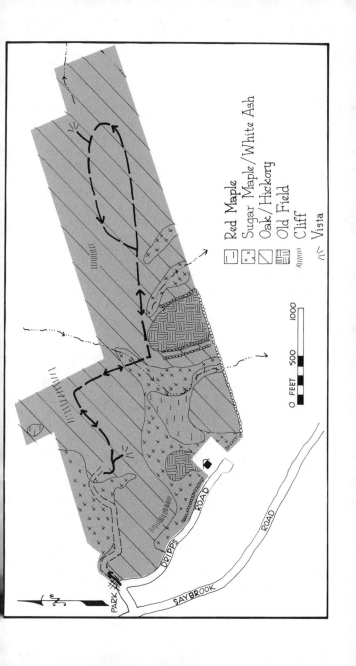

Red Maple
Sugar Maple/White Ash
Oak/Hickory
Old Field
Cliff
Vista

0 FEET 500 1000

N

PARK
DRIPPS ROAD
SAYBROOK ROAD

vegetation communities.) Both pines and cedars do well in these nutrient-poor mineral soils, although in 1985 Hurricane Gloria toppled some of these trees and opened up the view. Tucked in the moist fissures of rock are lush mosses and grasses. Shrubs are primarily low blueberry.

The southerly aspect of the land directs the eye to hay fields mantling a gently rounded hill. Unfortunately, the view is less than perfect, given the constant stream of traffic on Route 9. Keep an eye out for turkey vultures, which can often be seen from the opening.

Return to the old road heading east and follow the white blazes under massive rock outcrops. Look for the double blaze indicating a right-hand turn and follow the trail downhill to the brook.

The road at the base of the pegmatite cliffs gives wonderful views of these towering rocks. It is easy to imagine Indians making camp beneath the broad ledges and keeping watch from the cliffs over the surrounding land below. The summit of Bear Hill (660 feet) is located just to the north (off Conservancy property). It is crossed by the Mattabesett Trail, which connects the Conservancy's Higby Mountain Preserve in Middletown with Bluff Head in North Guilford.

The trail leading downhill beneath a series of parallel ledges crosses deeper, potassium-rich soils. The oaks in this moist habitat are some of the largest on the preserve. In spring, vernal pools form at the top of these ledges. Important in the life cycles of woodland frogs and salamanders, by summer's end these pools will be totally dry. In the early spring, look for bloodroot and trillium. Jack-in-the-pulpit and wild geranium are both common.

The dry oak-hickory forest of the upper slopes grades into richer woods by the stream. The maple-leaved viburnum of the midslopes gives way to a thick cover of mountain laurel flanking the stream. The trail detours around many trees that fell when this south-facing slope experienced the full force of Hurricane Gloria. The opened areas are now filled with panic grass, a broad-bladed species that typically becomes established on disturbed sites.

Cross the stream (sometimes dry) and follow the blazed trail to an old farm lane. Turn left and follow the lane due east. (Please note that the abandoned lane to the west enters private property and has been closed.) Farther along, where the double blazes indicate the loop trail, continue straight ahead.

The lane used to connect the preserve donor's house and barn on Dripps Road (to the west) with the pasture land (to the east). This same road once continued farther east to the former fishing village known as Maromas, at the southern end of Middletown and on the Connecticut River. The settlement was bought by the Connecticut Atomic Nuclear Energy Laboratory, which razed the houses and set up shop for a short time. The plant was subsequently taken over by Pratt and Whitney, a major aircraft manufacturer which is now a part of United Technologies.

The lane runs along stone walls demarcating pastures once used for hay and grazing of livestock. The old barways you'll see still hold the durable American chestnut split rails. These areas are now filled with mixed hardwoods which have over-topped the red cedar—the first species to invade abandoned fields. The trees growing along the lane are good indicators of the soil types. Large, well-formed maples, oaks and black birches grow on the better-drained sites, while tulip trees do well at the edge of more poorly-drained, wet soils. The multiple trunks of the tulip trees are probably the result of a fire or logging operation. The healthy roots of the severed tree continue to nourish the stump, which in turn sends up dozens of sprouts. Over time these sprouts compete for sunlight, with only the strongest three or four stems surviving to create the tree form we see today.

The trail climbs steeply through rock outcrops and mountain laurel, then bends left to head back in a westerly direction. A long spur-trail (about half a mile) leads farther uphill (bearing right off the main trail and marked by yellow blazes) to another overlook. After admiring the view, retrace your footsteps to the main loop-trail that joins the old farm lane, where you turn right at the double blazes. Retrace your steps down the lane, turn right uphill to the area of the first lookout, then downhill to your parked car.

In 1967, Helen Lohman donated 150 acres to the Conservancy for Spiderweed. She claims to have named her property to reflect the sad state in which she found her gardens each spring.

20

ST. JOHNS LEDGES

Kent

*Walking—1 mile round-trip to the top of the ledges
via a steep stone staircase. At the top is a splendid view
of the Housatonic River and surrounding land. An
additional 5-mile hike north on the Appalachian Trail
follows the west bank of the Housatonic River and
makes easy walking.*

---

*DIRECTIONS: From the center of Kent on Route
7, go west on Route 341 across the Housatonic River.
Take an immediate right (north) on Skiff Mountain
Road past the Kent School fieldhouse and proceed
north along the river for 1.1 miles. Bear right on
River Road which turns to dirt, and continue north
for 1.7 miles to the trailhead at the foot of St. Johns
Ledges. The Appalachian Trail is clearly marked by
white blazes.*

*To drop an extra car at the northern end of this
section of trail, return to Kent and drive north
on Route 7 to Cornwall Bridge (7.5 miles). Once
across the high concrete bridge in Sharon, take an
immediate right down under the bridge. Head south
along the Housatonic River for 1.4 miles. Park at
the junction of River Road, Dawn Hill Road, and
Guinea Road.*

OWNERSHIP OF THE LEDGES has been traced back to the beginning of the eighteenth century when the Schaghticoke Indians held the land on the west side of the Housatonic River. Subsequently, Kent was organized (1783), and the northern section of the Indian territory was sold to John Fuller. Fifty years later, Fuller sold this land to Timothy St. Johns, whose name remains with the ledges.

The land records are not clear from 1833 until 1910, when The Stanley Works of New Britain began purchasing large tracts of land on either side of the Housatonic in preparation for damming the river. The dam has yet to be built. In 1976, the company gave 132 acres, including St. Johns Ledges, to The Nature Conservancy and also granted an easement over the part of the Appalachian Trail that runs north into Sharon, following the western bank of the river—a fine example of an industry acting responsibly toward the environment and for the public benefit. In 1985, the Conservancy sold this tract to the U.S. National Park Service (NPS), while The Stanley Works conveyed additional sections of the Appalachian Trail Corridor to the NPS, which now owns and maintains the trail. Of the two thousand miles of trail stretching from Georgia to Maine, this stretch along the Housatonic River is considered by many to be the jewel in the crown.

Follow the trail into the woods in a northwestern direction. The trail soon swings to the south and begins a steep climb over occasional loose stones. Watch your footing. This section of trail has an occasional trouble spot over which the hiker must proceed with caution.

The first leg of the trail leads through mixed hardwoods, predominantly red oaks. The understory is dogwood, with

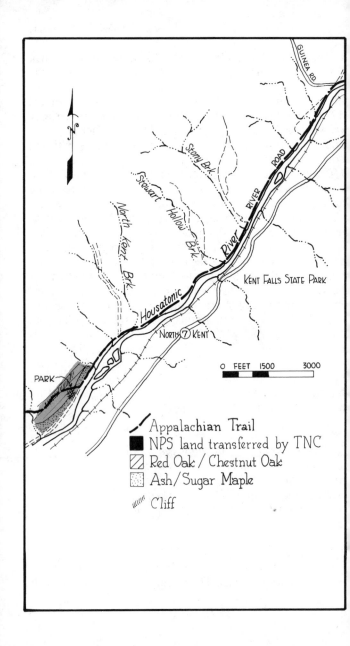

N

Appalachian Trail
NPS land transferred by TNC
Red Oak / Chestnut Oak
Ash / Sugar Maple
Cliff

GUINEA RD.

Stony Brk.

Stewart Hollow Brk.

North Kent Brk.

RIVER ROAD

Housatonic River

KENT FALLS STATE PARK

NORTH 7 KENT

PARK

0   FEET   1500   3000

witch hazel and maple-leaved viburnum in the shrub stratum. The red oaks at the base of the mountain are better developed than the chestnut oaks at the top of the ledges, reflecting the superior growing conditions of the lower woods. On the gentle lower slopes the soil is held in deeper pockets, with richer nutrients and far more moisture than the thin droughty soils of the summit. A woodsman must marvel at the well-formed, straight oaks lining River Road. Their proximity to the road in so remote an area apparently creates a situation conducive to wood-poaching. Indeed, several ash trees have been cut recently from along the road.

The switchback brings the trail across an area that soil scientists call rock land. Large boulders are jammed together, and the sparse soils caught between them appear to have been inadequate to support the forest vegetation. Probably drought and gypsy-moth caterpillars combined to kill the trees. A quick glance shows that there are as many dead trees toppled over as there are live ones still standing. In contrast, the herbaceous layer is well developed, with interrupted ferns on the left of the trail—"interrupted" because the fertile leaflets occur halfway along the arching, leafy frond—and delicate maidenhair ferns on the right.

The trail continues directly under sheer cliffs that rise sixty to eighty feet overhead. These cliffs mark the eastern boundary of the Housatonic Highlands Massif, one of the oldest bedrock formations in New England, with gneiss dating from the Precambrian Period over one billion years ago. From across the river, these ledges that rise five hundred to six hundred feet above the Housatonic River are clearly distinguishable, along with mountain summits that rise yet another three hundred feet.

Downhill from the trail, the forest is noticeably void of undergrowth due to an early spring fire several years ago. The fire swept along the base of the ledges, destroying many of the younger maple and ash trees that now can be seen sprouting anew. The oaks, with their thicker bark, withstood the heat and continue to flourish. Increased numbers of raspberry and blackberry bushes also grow in the wake of the fire. Fire continues to be a problem along the western bank of the Housatonic because of the many camping areas developed at the river's edge. The valley acts as a kind of funnel for wind currents that can fan even campfires out of control.

The cliffs are almost bare. A variety of lichens encrust the steep pitches and turn the gray gneiss slightly green or brown. Black birches take root in crevices where soil accumulates and moisture is trapped. Chestnut oaks and an occasional mountain laurel grow in slightly deeper pockets of soils and, where the trail climbs through a moister break in the rock, basswood, a species typically associated with stream banks, can be observed. Here, too, is the lovely, purple-flowering raspberry, with its thornless, sticky-hairy reddish stem. Its showy flowers are in bloom during June.

The last leg of trail is an extraordinary climb up a long stone staircase that rises through one of the few breaks in the cliff face. At the top of the ledge, the trail leads south through vegetation dwarfed by the harsh climate on this exposed site. From the top of the ledges, the view of the Housatonic River Valley is superb. The river flows along the western edge of the narrow valley. The east bank is a series of terraces; the lower ones are used to grow crops or to graze dairy cattle. The houses of North Kent cluster below, and even the tiny cemetery stones are quite distinct from this vantage point. Those fields abandoned by farmers in the past twenty to fifty years are full of red cedar.

By the end of the nineteenth century, most of the forests in the Housatonic River Valley had been cut for charcoal to fire the large stone furnaces where iron was smelted. The upper slopes of the hillside opposite the lookout were among those logged to support the iron industry. The smelting furnaces can be visited to the north of Kent on Route 7.

*If you were to continue southwest along the
Appalachian Trail, you would enter Pond Mountain
Natural Area and climb Caleb's Peak (see Chapter
38). Instead, retrace your steps down St. Johns
Ledges to the car. If you plan to continue on the
longer hike north into Sharon, turn left and follow
River Road (and the white blazes of the Appalachian
Trail) upstream along the Housatonic.*

The stretch of road running half a mile in each direction
from the trail junction is noted by Noble Proctor to be
one of the "hot spots" in Connecticut birding. River
Road in Kent is highlighted in his book *25 Birding
Areas in Connecticut* as being especially exciting during
spring migration. Look for ospreys, red-tailed hawks, and
turkey vultures overhead, mallards, black ducks, and wood
ducks on the river and in backwaters. During migration
periods, common goldeneyes and American mergansers
may be seen. In May, the east-facing slope is alive with
warblers.

The road continues north another mile to the old North
Kent bridge abutment. It passes several cellar holes dating
from colonial times on the west side of the road, as well as
a few modern camping sites along the river bank. The old
sugar maples that line the road were planted a hundred
and fifty to two hundred years ago, and may last another
100 years.

*If you have driven this far, park here where it's easy
to turn around, and walk the rest of the way.*

The scenic Appalachian Trail leads the hiker through
a variety of forest types that line the Housatonic River.
Hemlocks grow along the river's tributaries, and mixed

hardwoods and occasional grassy openings occur along the route, as do a few conifer plantations. The Housatonic River, though, is the major attraction. It rises near Pittsfield, Massachusetts, and flows south past Great Barrington and into Connecticut. From Kent, its most western point, the river swings southeast through New Milford to Derby and empties into Long Island Sound at Stratford and Milford—past the Conservancy's Milford Point. (See chapter 33.) It's a 132-mile trip through a mosaic of forests and agricultural land dotted with towns and villages.

Here at Kent, the quality of the Housatonic River water was once rated class "B"—suitable for swimming, boating, and fishing. In 1976, however, the river was downgraded to class "D" because of high levels of polychlorinated biphenols (PCBs) in its fish. Efforts continue to return the waters to their original class "B" rating and to designate a forty-one–mile segment of the Housatonic (from the Massachusetts–Connecticut border to New Milford) as a National Wild and Scenic River.

At the northern end of the road, the trail follows the river, passing an opening to cultivated fields. Continue to follow the white blazes of the Appalachian Trail. The trail joins a farm road to the north of an old foundation and continues past a spring that has been piped out to the edge of the road. The parking spot for a second car is a few hundred feet farther on.

21

STILL POND

Greenwich

Walking—Less than a mile. This small natural area of great charm and beauty is perfect for children, since the paths are broad and run beside two ponds, waterfalls, and streams. The woods are mature beech, oak, and sugar maple. In season, you can usually spot a wood duck or a mallard on Meek Pond.

DIRECTIONS: From the north: take the Merritt Parkway to Greenwich, take exit 31, and go south on North Street for 2.6 miles to Doubling Road on the left.

From the south: take the Boston Post Road to Greenwich, turn north onto North Street, and continue for 1.7 miles to Doubling Road on the right.

Follow Doubling Road for 0.5 mile. Turn left on Saw Mill Lane and continue for 0.3 mile. Pull into #31 driveway. On the right-hand side of the driveway, just before the culvert, parking space is provided for two cars.

THE PRESERVE AT STILL POND is typical of Greenwich's hilly terrain, remarkably sculpted by scouring glaciers some fifteen thousand years ago. Bedrock

outcrops are common along the ridges, while wetlands and ponds occupy the depressions. Still Pond has been dammed since colonial times and for decades provided ice, which was stored in the adjacent icehouse.

Follow the path from the parking place along a narrow, intermittent stream to Still Pond. Cross the bridge leading past the pond's outlet.

The woods on the left (north) of the trail and across the wet area are primarily large sugar maples and ashes growing on the rocky upland overlooking the pond. South of the trail is what appears to be an old well, partially filled with soil and framed in rock at the edge of a small wetland supporting red maples and sizable swamp white oaks. Skunk cabbages carpet the mucky ground. Except for the American chestnuts that were salvaged in the early decades of the twentieth century, the woods at Still Pond have been left more or less intact, and the trees are now sixty or seventy feet tall. The stone foundation and chimneys to the north of the trail are all that remain of a small cottage, last inhabited fifty years ago. No one locally quite knows its history but, once destroyed, it was never restored.

The icehouse farther along the trail has fared better. The building has been registered as a historical landmark by the Greenwich Historical Society. According to a local historian, it may well have begun as a root cellar, since the second story is clearly a later addition. The ground floor was constructed from local fieldstone at two separate periods. The inside wall was carefully laid with mortar in the mid-nineteenth century or earlier. The outside layer dates from a more recent time; it was probably added to give structural support for the second story. This upper wall is stucco on the outside and handsome wood paneling on

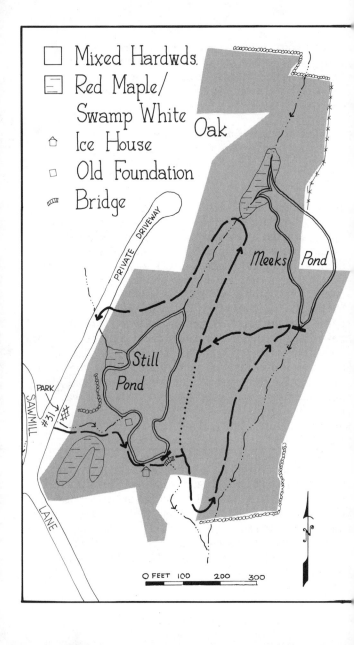

Mixed Hardwds.

Red Maple/
Swamp White Oak

Ice House

Old Foundation

Bridge

PRIVATE DRIVEWAY

Meeks Pond

Still Pond

PARK

#31

SAWMILL

LANE

0 FEET 100   200   300

N

the inside. Only remnants of the inner wall are still visible. The walls were insulated by filling the spaces between the studs with sawdust. Sawdust was also layered between the blocks of ice to retard melting during the hot summer months. The icehouse currently is maintained by the preserve committee. In the past a local collector of antique ice-cutting equipment demonstrated the art of ice harvesting.

Once across the pond's outlet, turn right and follow the path south for a short distance along the stream. The trail swings east, crossing the upper reaches of a small wetland, and then proceeds north (for a short distance on private property protected by a conservation easement) to the cinder-block dam at the end of Meek Pond. Cross the dam and loop back to Still Pond.

The high ground between Still Pond and Meek Pond is underlain by bedrock of schist and gneiss which is exposed along several north–south trending ridges. This well-drained upland supports a mature mixed-hardwood forest with oaks and beeches dominant in the canopy, and maple-leaved viburnum and dogwood beneath. Notice the grove on the west-facing slope adjacent to Still Pond, where beeches of all sizes grow to the near-exclusion of other species. The younger trees are root suckers, having originated from the root systems of mature trees in the area.

Another curiosity linked directly with the beech is the beech drop. These tan-colored parasites, growing to a height of six to eight inches, are quite common. Instead of producing chlorophyll to grow, they get most of their nutrients directly from the host beech. You may see their whitish flowers in the autumn.

Meek Pond is a recent creation: surface waters of a for
mer swamp were dammed to raise the water level by a
couple of feet. With the addition of nesting boxes, wood
ducks have been attracted to this shallow pond. Mallard
also frequent Meek Pond. There is a good view of both
pond and ducks (in the spring) from the western bank.

Once on the trail bordering Still Pond, observe the sec
tions of an enormous tree trunk whose stump is almost
yard in diameter. The giant American chestnut was a major
component of the oak forest covering the Eastern United
States until a widespread blight devastated its population
in the early part of this century, and it disappeared from
New England forests. The few chestnuts left standing even
tually died and tumbled over. Here, where the trunk has
been sawed in pieces, the hiker can still see the radiating
growth pattern of these very tough, rot-resistant trees.

The trail is just broad enough to let sunlight reach the
forest floor and this, in turn, influences the growth of her
baceous vegetation. Typical woodland species such as wild
lily of the valley give way to species more common in open
fields, such as goldenrod. Along the mossy pond bank
the understory is dominated by large, flowering dogwood
which bloom in mid-May.

*Once across the wetland located north of Still Pond,
bear left and return to the paved driveway (turning
left again) and your car.*

The return trail passes through more rich, moist wood
dominated by sugar maples and oaks with an occasiona
tulip tree at the edge of the wetland. In spring, the skun
cabbages growing along the stream are intermixed with
daffodils, obvious escapees from neighboring property.

The path joins the driveway at the point where
Rockwood Lake Brook crosses under the road an

empties into Still Pond. Upstream and off Conservancy property, the brook tumbles over shiny black slabs of bedrock flanked by Christmas ferns. The walk back to the car is quiet except for the breeze that hisses incessantly through the red pines planted on the left-hand side of the road. Although the preserve at Still Pond is small, its many visitors are impressed by its charm, serenity, and interesting history.

The Conservancy acquired this preserve through transactions, part sale and part gift, known as bargain sales. Thirteen acres came from Ann H. Shellenberger, and four and a half acres from Priscilla M. Meek. A scenic easement over almost an acre was donated by Mr. and Mrs. John Hill Wilson.

22

TURTLE CREEK

Essex and Old Saybrook

Walking—About a mile through mountain-laurel thickets and beech groves, under dense hemlock, and out along one of the Connecticut River's coves.

DIRECTIONS: From Middletown take Route 9 south to exit 2. (From I-95 go north on Route 9 to exit 2.) Turn north on Route 154 (Middlesex Turnpike) and proceed for 0.8 mile. Turn right on Watrous Point Road. The entrance and parking area lie on the left in 0.2 mile.

ROUTE 9, the Chester Bowles Turnpike, will bring you part of the way to Turtle Creek, which is appropriate since the late Governor and Mrs. Bowles donated most of the land in this ninety-three–acre wildlife sanctuary. Straddling the Essex–Old Saybrook town line, the preserve occupies the mouth of Turtle Creek, a tidal estuary whose channel supports wild rice and eel grass. The well-developed trail system runs through hemlock, oak, and hickory stands and old fields. You can catch a glimpse of Essex, home of the Dickinson Witch Hazel Company, from the beach at South Cove.

*Although the main trail lies dead ahead of the
parking area, take an immediate right and follow a
narrow trail (all trails here have yellow blazes) that
parallels Watrous Point Road in an easterly direction.
The trail runs through hemlocks and mountain laurel
and descends a slight incline past a large boulder on
your right.*

The bedrock underlying the preserve is composed of
gneisses and schists approximately 460 million years old,
but it is the overlying mantle of glacial deposits that has
had a greater influence on the preserve's soil formation
and vegetation distribution. The Connecticut River basin
was filled with ice about thirteen thousand years ago. As
the ice cap melted, rock particles of all sizes that had
been scoured from the earth's surface were deposited
throughout the area. One large boulder, transported by
the ice flow, came to rest on this slope. It is known as a
glacial erratic. You'll see clusters of erratics as you continue
your walk through the woods.

If you make this walk in the fall or winter, you also
may see the tan egg cases of the gypsy moth. In the
summers of 1981 and 1982, many of the forests in this
region were defoliated by gypsy-moth caterpillars. The
tiny, innocent-looking larvae hatch in the warmth of late
spring and begin to chew their way through the canopy.
As they munch—first on the oaks and maples, then
on the birches and beeches, and finally on the pines
and hemlocks—they grow steadily larger (to almost
three inches) and ultimately eat all available food. As
a result, the forests are denuded and give us the eerie
sensation of spring where there should be summer. Their
food source depleted, the caterpillars form cocoons and
pupate, emerging as small moths. The males, which are
light brown, are able to fly, but the white females can only
flutter and drift (sometimes long distances) in the wind as

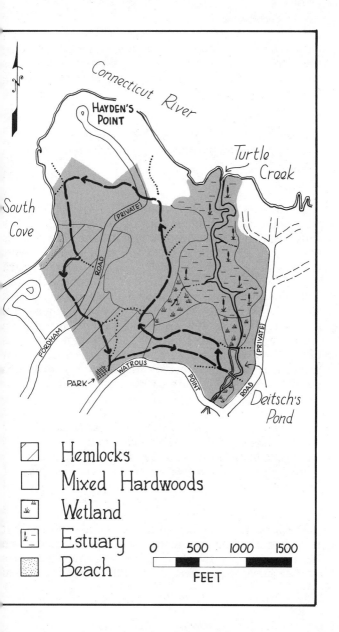

Connecticut River

HAYDEN'S POINT

Turtle Creek

South Cove

ROAD (PRIVATE)

FORDHAM

PARK →

WATROUS

POINT

ROAD (PRIVATE)

Deitsch's Pond

▨ Hemlocks
☐ Mixed Hardwoods
🌱 Wetland
↓⁻ Estuary
▦ Beach

0   500   1000   1500

FEET

they wait for a male. Once the female moths are fertilized, they lay hundreds of eggs in fawn-colored masses along tree trunks for next spring's crop of young caterpillars.

Leaving the glacial erratic behind, cross the main trail and continue straight ahead for a glimpse of Deitsch's Pond.

The descent to Deitsch's Pond, built for ice production by William Deitsch at the turn of the century, is heavy with the scent of sweet pepperbush in June. The pond is filling in rapidly to the south, where suspended sediments brought downstream by a relatively swift current reach the wide banks and still waters of the pond and sink. The newly created sandbar supports swamp species such as purple loosestrife, jewelweed, and skunk cabbage. In the summer months, if you approach the pond quietly, you are apt to spot basking turtles. The northern two-thirds of the pond remain more open. As you can see, the few planks that once constituted a bridge across a small dam are not to be trusted. Turn back!

Retrace your steps and go right at the intersection below the glacial erratic. The trail parallels the shoreline of the pond. Bear left on the trail as you pass under the power line, and follow it until it joins the main trail.

This section of trail is a special delight to children, as it leads into a meandering tunnel of mountain laurel which blooms in early to mid-June. Look closely at the flowers and see how they are fertilized. Each stamen is released from a tiny pocket in the flower when agitated by a bee (or your finger) and springs forward, dousing the intruder with pollen.

Sadly, the beech trees have been carved to a fare-thee-well. The humor of "everyone writes on trees but me," appearing on one fallen tree, is lost on most people who enjoy these woods. This tree, upturned by the 1954 hurricane and still quite alive, sports an earlier inscription that is now sideways. Later graffiti, carved after the tree fell, runs upright along the length of the trunk.

Notice the great number of small beech trees in this section of the preserve. Beech propagates via root suckers. The nourishment stored in a mature tree goes, in part, to stimulate the growth of new beech sprouts, often leaving little room for any other species.

The trail skirts a narrow depression formed by a spring or seep. Archaeologists believe that the Indians inhabiting Hayden's Point probably lived within a hundred yards of this spring for its year-round fresh water supply. The moist ground supports a lush patch of shiny clubmoss (*Lycopodium lucidulum*). The Nature Conservancy established a permanent study transect here in 1978 to determine the rate of erosion. Other permanent research plots have been placed along slopes throughout the preserve.

Go right and follow the main trail. A spur trail marked "Marsh" leads downhill on the right for an imperfect view of the wetland. Follow the main trail as it swings away from the wetland and eventually reaches an asphalt road. Continue straight across the road and follow the trail toward South Cove.

On the glacial terraces that form Hayden's Point lie a series of fields—some still open, others filling in with woody species. At the turn of the century the point was grazed, and the area supported grasses. Shortly thereafter, the pastures were abandoned, and the first red cedars moved in. If you were to count their annual rings, you would discover that the trees are seventy years old. They are now dead or dying, crowded out by other, more shade-tolerant species, such as oak. The black birch is another tree that does well in full sunlight. Longer-lived than cedar, and growing taller so that it can take more advantage of the sunlight, the black birch continues to dominate in this transitional forest. The green understory is a tangle of thorny greenbrier and bittersweet; clubmosses cover the forest floor. Closer to the water, notice the occasional large oak and numerous beeches. This is the one area to beware of poison ivy, distinguished by its three-leaf clusters.

At the top of South Cove bank, go left. Please don't clamber down the bank; instead, use the built-in log steps that help protect against erosion to get to the beach below.

Looking northwest across the cove, you can see the spires of the churches in Essex. During the eighteenth and nineteenth centuries, Essex was well known for its ship-building and lumbering operations. The Hayden family, for which the point is named, owned many of Essex's business enterprises and residences. The eighteenth and nineteenth centuries were also a time when shad were plentiful in the Connecticut River and commercially important. Check the shallows of the cove for ducks, waders, and swans.

Continue south along the rim of South Cove. After an old logging road joins the trail from the left, bear

right and enter the dark shadows under the hemlocks.
Follow this trail as it recrosses the asphalt road and
continue south (bearing right where the trail splits) to
the parking area.

The western section of the wildlife sanctuary supports a
hemlock forest of special beauty. The hemlock has become
an increasingly important component of the forest here as
natural fires have been prevented. Data gathered from
a permanent study plot suggest that the hemlocks are
extending their range to the north and east in the preserve
and that, given the absence of fire, they are likely to
continue to spread.

If, however, the hemlock become infested with the hemlock woolly adelgid, we may witness a complete die-back
of the tree species. This insect has become a serious pest
since 1985 when Hurricane Gloria transported the adelgids
across Long Island Sound. Its egg masses, covered with
a secreted, white woolly substance, hatch in the spring.
Within days, the young begin feeding on the hemlock and
quickly weaken the tree by removing sap and injecting a
toxic spittle. Adelgids are capable of killing a mature tree
within one year. If this should happen at Turtle Creek,
the whole aspect of the woods will be altered. The prob-
able result will be a mixed-hardwood forest where oaks
are dominant.

In the springtime, keep a keen eye to the east of the trail.
Just shy of the parking area are clumps of pink lady's slipper, a handsome large pink orchid. Look closely—you
also may find only a hole where the plant used to be. Of
all the management problems facing the Conservancy's local stewardship committee, none is as disheartening and as
hard to solve as flower-robbing. Trowels have no place in
a nature preserve.

The late Governor and Mrs. Chester Bowles donated most of the Turtle Creek Wildlife Sanctuary to The Nature Conservancy over a thirteen-year period. More recent gifts of land came from Oliver May and Charles and Dorothy Mills.

23

WEIR NATURE PRESERVE

Wilton

*Walking—2 miles or less on a well-marked trail
that leads over ledges, past cascading water, along
a wetland, through mountain laurel, and across open
fields.*

---

*DIRECTIONS: From Wilton center, go north on
Route 33 for 2 miles, then turn right onto Nod Hill
Road. The entrance is 3.3 miles down the road,
on the left. From Ridgefield, go south on Route 33
(Main Street). Turn left on Route 102 and continue
for 1.2 miles. Turn right on Nod Road and go for 1.6
miles. Soon after crossing the Ridgefield–Wilton town
line, turn left on Pelham Lane. At the far end, turn
right on Nod Hill Road and continue for 0.4 mile.
The entrance is on the right. There is limited parking
in the old lane.*

THE WEIR NATURE PRESERVE now comprises 110
acres, including woodlots, wetlands, and upland once
cleared for agriculture. For the most part, the soils are
shallow to bedrock and of little value for cultivation. The
old fields along Pelham Lane to the north have been
allowed to revert to woodland, while others along Nod

Hill are still mown. Within the preserve's boundaries, two wetlands drain into Comstock Brook.

From the Nod Hill Road entrance, between two stone walls, follow the yellow blazes along the old farm track. Check the trail-system map on the entrance sign set back four or five hundred feet from the road. The yellow-blazed trail system transects the central portion of the preserve, while the blue blazes mark the main southern trail. The red blazes mark the northwestern loop and the white blazes the northeastern loop interpretive trail. Green and orange have been used for the southern trails, which are connected via the blue trail to Turtleback Road. A handsome and informative guidebook is available (for a donation) from the Weir Preserve Committee at P.O. Box 7033, Wilton, CT 06897.

The Weir Preserve is underlain by gneisses and granites and includes numerous outcrops. The stone walls of the area are especially handsome, as are the stone bridges that cross most streams. Some of the ledges were quarried to provide foundation stones for nearby structures and granite paving slabs.

A thick growth of Christmas ferns that stay green all winter long flank the roadway. In spring and summer, their ranks swell with numerous other fern species, including broad beech, crested wood, and marginal shield ferns on upland sites, and cinnamon, sensitive, and royal ferns in wetter areas.

The forest is mixed hardwoods, primarily oak and hickory with some maple and beech. The understory is mountain laurel on the well-drained sites. The black birch is also a component of this forest and most probably seeded in when the fields were abandoned, close to

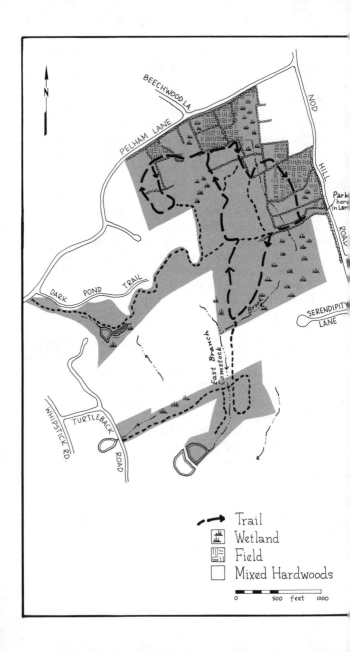

N

BEECHWOOD LA.

PELHAM LANE

NOD

HILL

Park
here
in Lane

ROAD

DARK POND TRAIL

SERENDIPITY LANE

Brook

East Branch Comstock

WHIPSTICK RD.

TURTLEBACK ROAD

→ Trail

Wetland

Field

Mixed Hardwoods

0   500 feet 1000

the turn of the century. This drier forest grades into red maple, tulip poplar, and yellow birch, with a thick shrub stratum of spicebush in the wetlands.

Where the undergrowth is thick, especially in the mountain laurel groves, expect to be startled by the explosive takeoff of a ruffed grouse or two. Somewhat secretive, they scratch in the leaves in search of seeds and insects and fly off only at the very last moment.

Shortly, following the second stone stream-crossing on the farm track (about 700 feet from the Nod Hill Road entrance), look for a blue blaze on the left that leads through a break in the stone wall. This is the southern loop trail—well worth the trip.

The blue blazes lead through a carpet of clubmoss, generally thought to indicate past grazing. The path climbs gently to the top of a short but steep rise. At the foot, the upper limit of the wetland, there are enormous red oaks, one nearly four feet in diameter. From here, in winter, there are nice views across the swamp, and in spring, peepers fill the air. The path has been clipped through mountain laurel and shows their crooked growing pattern to great effect. Also watch for an unusually large, four-inch striped maple alongside the path.

The trail reaches a broad ledge adjacent to a brook that comes tumbling over a series of rock outcrops. Common polypody and mosses thrive in this cool, moist habitat. The ledge has excellent views to the south and west. Here you can either continue south on the blue trail or loop back via the blue-yellow trail, following this guide.

The return trail follows the western edge of the ridge back through dense mountain laurel. The excessively drained soils support large chestnut oaks. These trees must have been cut at an earlier date, or buried, which would explain their multiple stump sprouts. Note the one curious, small opening in the "monoculture" of mountain laurel, which is filled with sweet pepperbush. Perhaps its occurrence is best explained by a seep or spring in the underlying bedrock.

Turn left onto the yellow-blazed trail and proceed along the eastern side of the wetland. Once at the beech grove, bear uphill and out to Pelham Lane, or bear left on the red-blazed loop trail.

The Weir Preserve is dominated by oaks, so it is somewhat startling to find a grove of beeches with gray trunks turning soft silver in sunlight. The west-facing bowl of deeper, richer soils supports large beeches, one or two of which have unfortunately been carved by neighborhood children. In the spring, the pale green leaves of the beech cause an unreal light to filter through the forest. And in late fall, when most other trees have lost their leaves, the dry, pale-yellow beech leaves flicker in the afternoon light.

The red-blazed trail climbs through a stone wall at an old dump site. Watch your footing. The trail recrosses the same stone wall to avoid a swampy spot and passes just below a spring and a huge white oak. The red blazes lead through an old field and over ledges at the extreme western section of the preserve; they then loop back east. Bear left along the red-blazed trail at both junctions with the red-yellow trail.

The old field has reverted to woodland dominated by black birches. The forest floor is covered in clubmosses. In early spring, expect to find bloodroot and Dutchman'sbreeches, and look later for red trillium, columbine, and lady's slipper. The rocky terrain of the loop boasts large glacial erratics scattered across the steep slope, while the dry ridge top is dominated by chestnut oaks.

Once you have rejoined the yellow-blazed trail, turn right and head south through the old field. After 200 feet, bear left and follow the yellow-white blazes. At the junction with the white trail, you may bear either left or right—both directions lead back to the yellow trail and out to the Nod Hill Road entrance sign. Turn left to reach your car.

The fields in the northern portion of the Weir Preserve are now filled with blueberry bushes, red cedars, junipers, and gray birches. The tawny grass, little bluestem, is indigenous and characteristic of many old fields in southern Connecticut. Cherry, oak, and sassafras are also moving into this area. These fields will be left to grow to forest.

On the far side of the stream, the fields are mown annually, avoiding the few standing red cedars. The cedars are pruned by deer that browse the area. Other wildlife that have been spotted include foxes and raccoons.

Only one hike through the Weir Preserve has been described here, but there are many more for return trips. The southern section is well worth a visit, as is the newest addition to the west, where a yellow-blazed trail runs along Dark Pond and joins the "through" trail to the Nod Hill entrance.

The Weir Preserve has been over ten years in the making and still continues to grow with new acquisitions. It originated in 1969 with a gift of thirty-seven acres from Cora Weir Burlingham to honor her father, J. Alden Weir, a noted American impressionist painter who made his home at the farmhouse on the corner of Nod Hill Road and Pelham Lane. His original 150 acres were eventually divided among his children, with a portion given to The Nature Conservancy. Since 1970, the preserve has more than doubled in size, with gifts from Eugenia Slaughter, in memory of George Leary; from Geoffrey and Elizabeth Baker, in memory of Anna White; and from Roger Geffen, Elsie French, and Helen Littauer.

24

WOLFPITS

Bethel

Walking—About a mile through old fields now reverted to woodlands. Nice views from ledges (when trees are not in leaf) and a visit to an old feldspar mine highlight the walk. A small dammed pond, formed by Wolf Pit Brook, lies between the forest and a wet meadow.

DIRECTIONS: From Bethel go east (toward Newtown) on Route 302. Go south (right) on Route 58, and, in a little over 1 mile, turn left onto Sunset Hill Road. Immediately turn sharply left onto Wolf Pit Road. The preserve is on the right (east) side of the road.

THE NATURE PRESERVE AT WOLFPITS has a colorful past. During the Revolution, the western slope was apparently an encampment area, and during Prohibition stills were located here.

From Bethel's incorporation in 1759 until the Depression, hat-making was the major town industry. Small hat factories, called buckeyes, flourished in each neighborhood. One was located just southwest of the preserve at the junction of Wolf Pit and Sunset roads. Comb-making

was another Bethel-based industry. P.T. Barnum, of circus fame, was born in Bethel and began his career fashioning combs from cow horns at ten cents an hour.

Bethel was also cleared for dairy farming. Stone walls are still intact throughout the wooded sections of the preserve. (Take special note of the wall at the edge of the ledges.) By the turn of the century, the trees that had filled these pastures reached a size worth cutting. In 1910, Ferry Sawmill was established just outside the northeast corner of the preserve. Mr. Ferry, whose family has owned land adjacent to the preserve for five generations, remembers the area as forest that was logged for railroad ties. An old access road at the northern end of the preserve was used to remove timber and quarry products.

Follow the path through the field to the pond's edge.

The western end of the preserve has been under the most recent cultivation. The southwest-corner lot was planted as an ornamental orchard with a variety of fruit trees—grown more for their flowers than for their fruit. The northern end of this lot was planted in conifers, both spruce and pine.

The pond was once filled ingeniously by way of an underground sluice which is now plugged by sand washed down from upstream development. The pond itself used to be considerably deeper and served as the neighborhood swimming hole. However, in the name of safety, its previous owner (Miss Janet Taylor) decided against allowing public use, and had the pond partially drained—a practical solution that the Conservancy still follows. The shallow water attracts birds and frogs, and greatly enhances the diversity of the preserve.

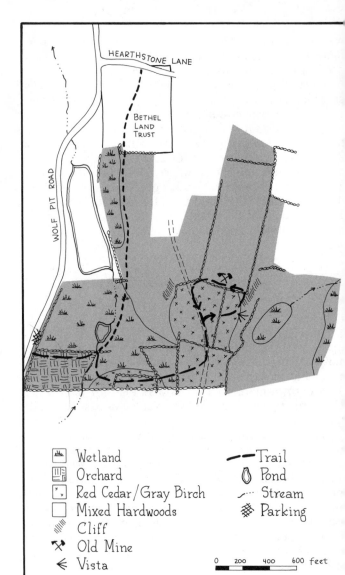

HEARTHSTONE LANE

WOLF PIT ROAD

BETHEL
LAND
TRUST

	Wetland		Trail
	Orchard		Pond
	Red Cedar/Gray Birch		Stream
	Mixed Hardwoods		Parking
	Cliff		
	Old Mine		
	Vista		

0   200   400   600 feet

For botanists, the wet meadow beyond the pond has special appeal. It supports a variety of ferns, including marsh, sensitive, and royal. This meadow is fast developing into a red-maple swamp with abundant pussywillow. The tussock sedge has given footing to shrubs such as steeplebushes and narrow-leaved dogwoods, as well as to young red maples, alders, and willows.

Wolf Pit Brook used to meander freely across the flat lowland, periodically depositing silt and clay transported in times of flood. This rich bottom land was valuable to local farmers, who rerouted the stream to flow along the edge of the meadow. A deer run, worth exploring, parallels this stretch of water.

Retrace your steps. Approximately 150 feet south of the pond, a trail leads across a simple plank bridge over Wolf Pit Brook and follows it upstream for a short distance. This trail is marked with yellow paint. (Two painted markings indicate a turn.) The trail swings east along the southern boundary of the preserve.

The west-facing slope was once cleared for pasturing animals. The incline is too steep for crops, but livestock could graze the area. The pastures, long since abandoned, have grown to forest. A conspicuous tree species, and one of the first to have invaded these fields, is red cedar. Here along the southern boundary it dominates the forest. It isn't often that one sees such healthy old specimens. The trees reach thirty feet and measure well over a foot in diameter. Beneath the cedars are highbush blueberry and witch hazels. Clubmosses, which indicate past grazing, and true mosses cover the forest floor. A garden escapee, winged euonymus, occurs occasionally beside the stream.

Shortly after crossing the second stone wall, look
for the yellow markings on a faint path bearing left
across a small wetland. Follow the trail uphill and
across a stone wall to the junction with a trail running
north–south.

The cedars give way to yellow birches in this swampy
spot. Along the slightly elevated eastern edge of the
wetland where the soil is better drained, the ground
is covered in trout lilies. This early spring wild flower
covers a wide area. Although there are numerous plants,
recognized by their splotchy green-brown leaves, there are
relatively few yellow blossoms. An individual plant blooms
only once every six or seven years.

The stone wall to the east of the wetland provides an
excellent illustration of a "slumping," or slowly eroding,
hillside. When it was first constructed, this wall, following the contour of the slope, measured approximately the
same height on its uphill and downhill sides. After the
forest upslope was logged, the entire hillside was open to
wholesale erosion. Upper layers of exposed soil washed
downhill where they were blocked by the stone wall. The
result is a half-buried wall that gives the appearance of a
terraced slope.

Turn north (left) at the junction of trails and cross
through a stone wall. Beyond, look for the yellow
blazes that lead to the right through another stone
wall. This trail leads out to the ledges.

The upper slopes of Wolfpits Nature Preserve overlie
Hollis and Charlton soils, characteristically rocky and
well- to excessively drained. They support a drier forest

whose canopy is dominated by white, black, and red oaks. Along the droughty hilltops, where the crystalline bedrock is exposed, the trees are poorly developed and chestnut oaks occur frequently. The understory and shrub strata of the oak forest are sparse to nonexistent, with flowering dogwood and maple-leaved viburnum most common. Low blueberry flanks the trail on these upper slopes.

The view from the ledges looks over an old, filled-in swamp or bog. When the leaves are off the trees, the bog is quite distinct from this distance, since it is filled with red maples that are rather stunted in comparison with the surrounding forest. The shrub layer—a mosaic of thickly growing sweet pepperbush, highbush blueberry, and swamp azalea—is also easy to distinguish.

Turn away from the top of the ledges, follow the yellow blazes westward to the quarry pit on the north side of the trail, and continue through a stone wall to a junction with another trail. Bear left and loop back to the original trail on which the hike began. Continue out of the woods to the car.

It's almost impossible to miss the opening to the abandoned feldspar mine, since the trail is strewn with chunks of sparkling white quartz. This mine was one of many that operated in the surrounding countryside. The feldspar, to be used in making porcelain and glass, was quarried from the gneissic bedrock. As evidenced by the debris on the trail, this mine obviously tapped a quartz vein, now well out of view under the collapsed mine walls. After the mine's abandonment, the forest reestablished itself. The slumping walls of the mine exposed mineral soils along the upper rim of the pit, where black birch seeds were able to germinate; along the lower flanks and basin, where richer organic soil readily developed, maple and ash took root. Today, some seventy years after the mine's closing, these trees have reached ten to twelve inches in diameter.

The preserve came to The Nature Conservancy in 1969 through the generosity of Miss Janet Taylor, who had acquired a large part of the preserve at a bargain. Unable to negotiate a deal with her neighbor, she finally bought the land through an intermediary. Sections of this parcel then passed back and forth between Miss Taylor and her neighbors, resulting in the odd configuration of the northern boundary.

SHORT HIKES

25

BALLYHACK

Cornwall

DIRECTIONS: From the junction of Routes 4 and 125 in Cornwall, proceed north on Route 125. The preserve's southern boundary lies approximately 1,000 feet north of the junction on the west side of the road. Continue about 0.5 mile farther north and turn west (left) on Dibble Hill Road. The entrance to the preserve is via a dirt road on the left, 500 feet from Route 125. Park at the edge of Dibble Hill Road.

BALLYHACK TODAY LOOKS very much as Cathedral Pines (a mile south) must have looked at the start of this century. (See chapter 6.) The preserve is dominated by mature white pines intermixed with hardwoods and hemlocks growing in a series of steep-sided ravines. It is located near the headwaters of Baldwin Brook, whose three branches run south through the preserve.

Access to the preserve is via Dibble Hill Road. Follow the road that marks the western boundary of Ballyhack and leads through the largest trees in the preserve situated along the rim of the ravine. The road, which bridges the deeply-cut streambed farther to the south, is flanked by stone walls.

Nancy Day Gillespie donated land for this preserve.

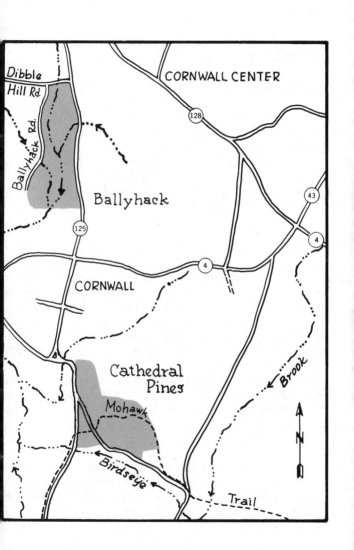

Dibble
Hill Rd.

CORNWALL CENTER

128

Ballyhack Rd.

Ballyhack

43

125

4

4

CORNWALL

Cathedral
Pines

Mohawk

Brook

Birdseye

Trail

N

26

BANTAM RIVER

Litchfield

DIRECTIONS: From the center of Litchfield, follow Route 202 toward Torrington (northeast) for a mile. Access is gained along a narrow strip of Conservancy-owned land on the western (left) side of Route 202 (adjacent to the Northwest Publishing Company property).

THE PRESERVE AT BANTAM RIVER occupies fifty-seven acres along the east bank of the Bantam River in Litchfield. Beavers have created several small reservoirs in the Bantam within the preserve's boundaries. A simple trail parallels the river and takes the hiker through vegetation typical of transitional hardwoods. The plants show northern affinities with species such as mountain maple and clintonia plus southern affinities with species such as oak and hickory. The old fields within the Bantam River Preserve have grown up in white pines, typical of the northern half of the state. Because the trail is close to the fluctuating waters of the Bantam River, visits to the preserve are more enjoyable in drier seasons.

Thomas C. Babbitt and Sherman Haight, Jr., donated land for this preserve. More than a hundred acres of additional land along the river is protected by conservation easements. Although these areas are not open to the public, the restrictions ensure protection of the watershed.

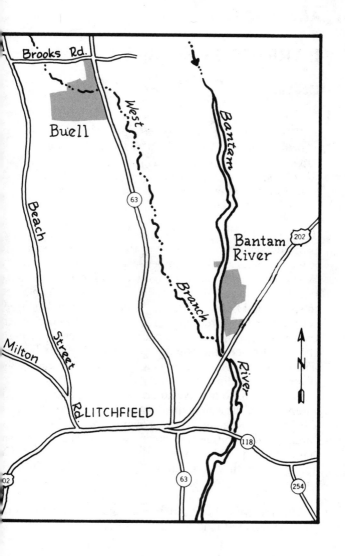

27

BARRETT PRESERVE

Ledyard

> *DIRECTIONS: From I-95, take exit 86 and go north on Route 12 toward Gales Ferry. In 3 miles go right on Long Cove Road. The preserve lies on the left-hand side of the road in 1 mile. The trail leads northwest just beyond the stand of conifers.*

IN THE PAST, its rocky character and steep slopes precluded cultivation of most of the Barrett Preserve, and it was last managed for timber at the turn of the century. A second-growth forest of oaks and hickories has since developed, and in 1954 a section of the land was planted in spruce and fir as a Christmas-tree plantation. The trees were never harvested and have now grown into a tightly packed stand. The eastern section of the preserve lies along the well-drained hilltop and is thick in huckleberry bushes. The open field is mown regularly, thereby increasing the diversity of wildlife.

Leading off Long Cove Road to the northeast of the conifers, a trail descends through the oak-hickory forest to Christie Hill Road and crosses over a stream where yellow birches and tulip trees are most common. The many dead hardwoods throughout the preserve resulted from two major gypsy-moth caterpillar infestations, one in 1966–67 and another in 1981–82.

Mr. and Mrs. Leighton Barrett and Marion Leighton Stubing donated land for this preserve.

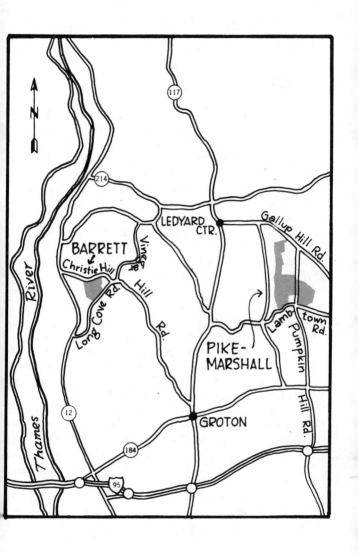

28

BLUFF HEAD

North Guilford

*DIRECTIONS: From Durham, take Route 17 south
and immediately bear left on Route 77 for 3.4 miles.
Turn right on Old Pent Road which is shortly after
Bluff Head Farm. Follow this right-of-way for 0.6
mile to the preserve and park. Please do not drive into
the preserve, and walk only on the trails.*

*From I-95, take exit 58 (Guilford) and follow Route
77 north for 9 miles. Old Pent Road is on the left.
In spring and after rains, this road is impassable. On
foot, follow Old Pent Road until it fords Hemlock
Brook. Take the next trail to the right.*

THE PRESERVE AT BLUFF HEAD is a seventy-five-
acre tract lying on the northeast slope and toe of a major
trap-rock ridge known as Totoket Mountain. Bluff Head is
a promontory at the top of steep cliffs overlooking a valley.
It lies outside the preserve boundaries but is protected by
the Guilford Land Conservation Trust.

A spur trail under the joint jurisdiction of the Trust and
the Conservancy leads westward, uphill through a mixed
hardwood and hemlock forest, and eventually onto Trust
owned property at the top of the ridge. Here the trail
intersects the Mattabessett Blue Trail and affords hikers
fine vistas.

The Nature Conservancy's Connecticut Chapter purchased Bluff Head in 1979 with a last-minute bid against
a developer who planned to subdivide the land.

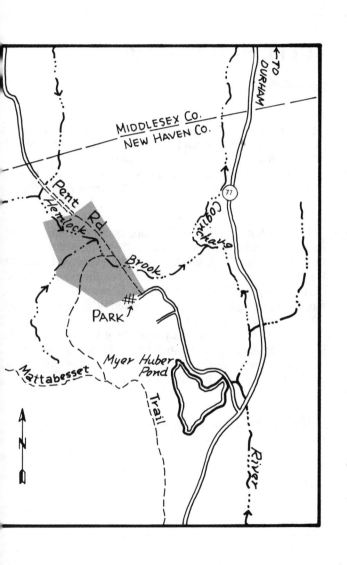

29

BUELL NATURAL AREA

Litchfield

DIRECTIONS: The preserve lies just south of the Goshen–Litchfield town line at the junction of Route 63 and Brooks Road, 3 miles north of Litchfield's center and 3 miles south of the center of Goshen. The trail leads from Brooks Road 300 feet from Route 63.

THE TOPOGRAPHY of the Buell Natural Area is gently rolling, typical of the elongated north-south trending hills, or drumlins, of Litchfield County. The preserve ranges in elevation from 1,040 to 1,200 feet and includes a scenic gorge cut by the West Branch of the Bantam River. Downstream the slope levels to a frequently flooded swamp where beavers are active.

A blazed trail leads south from Brooks Road and follows the contour of the south-facing slope. It runs west along the cascading West Branch of the Bantam River and provides one of the prettiest short hikes in the area.

Murray Buell and Zorac and Charlotte Organschi donated land for this preserve.

30

CURRIE MEMORIAL SANCTUARY

Kent

*DIRECTIONS: From Route 7 in Kent, follow
Route 341 west for 2.5 miles. The preserve lies on the
northern side of the road, partly in New York
State, partly in Connecticut. An old woods road leads
uphill into the preserve from the Connecticut end.*

SITUATED WEST OF THE HOUSATONIC RIVER
in the Housatonic Highlands, the Sanctuary covers a
very steep and rocky site with a southern exposure. It
is largely well drained on soils that, being shallow to
bedrock, support oaks and hickories with a ground cover
of huckleberries and blueberries. Along the ridgetop to
the northeast is a hop hornbeam (*Ostrya virginiana*)
community. Hornbeams take their name from their
European relatives that were used for yoking oxen.

In the nineteenth century, the entire area was cut over
for charcoal to fire iron furnaces. At lower elevations, numerous charcoal pits can still be detected. American chestnut was also salvaged from these hills during the second
decade of this century. An old logging road leaves Route
341 and cuts diagonally across the steep slope in the southern section of the preserve. The northeastern boundaries
of the preserve are shared with Macedonia Brook State
Park, through which the Appalachian Trail passes.

Dr. Bethia S. Currie donated land for this preserve.

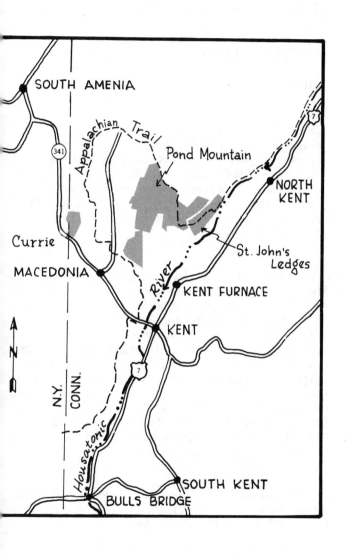

31

HAMLET HILL

Salisbury

DIRECTIONS: From Salisbury, take Route 44 north for 1 mile. The Appalachian Trail leads steeply up from the highway and runs the length of Patricia Winter Woodland Preserve, which was once the Conservancy's and is now owned and managed by the National Park Service. The trail continues through the preserve at Hamlet Hill and joins the dead-end of Sugar Hill Road.

WHAT WAS THE PATRICIA WINTER WOODLAND Preserve comprises 170 acres and is adjacent to the Conservancy's 365-acre preserve at Hamlet Hill. Both are situated on Wentauwanchu Mountain.

The preserve's terrain varies widely. A very steep slope with thin soils is dominated by hemlocks and rises to a plateau of postagricultural land characterized by ashes, birches, and sugar maples. The eastern and northern sections, through which the Appalachian Trail passes, have been logged more recently, and hemlock is interspersed here with mixed hardwoods. Steep ledges cut east–west through the center of Hamlet Hill, and there are several red-maple swamps in the preserve.

Donors of land for the preserve include Gustavus Pope, Agnes Forsyth, Mary McClintock, Henry Mitchell, John F. B. Mitchell, and Dorothy R. Walker.

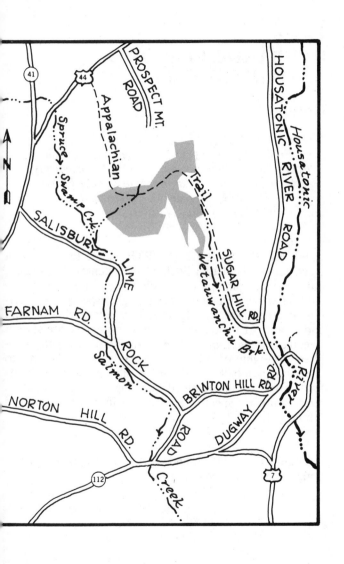

32

HUBBARD-DELACORTE NATURE PRESERVE

Greenwich

DIRECTIONS: Access to the preserve is poor along Weaver Street because of the swamp. Arrangements can be made to park in a private driveway. Please call The Nature Conservancy's Connecticut Chapter office for directions (203-344-0716).

THE HUBBARD-DELACORTE Nature Preserve is an eleven-acre island of wild land in a densely populated, quickly developing part of town. For its small size it provides an array of habitats that make it especially interesting. Two north-south ridges separate a low-lying wetland and brook. At the eastern end of the preserve are several sweetgum trees (*Liquidambar styracifina*). As its name implies, sweetgum trees exude a sticky sap that hardens into chewable gum balls. The tree is easily distinguished by its fruit: prickly, long-stemmed, hanging balls. Sweetgum, a more southerly species, approaches its northern limit in Greenwich.

Virginia Drake Horne and George and Valerie Delacorte donated land for this preserve.

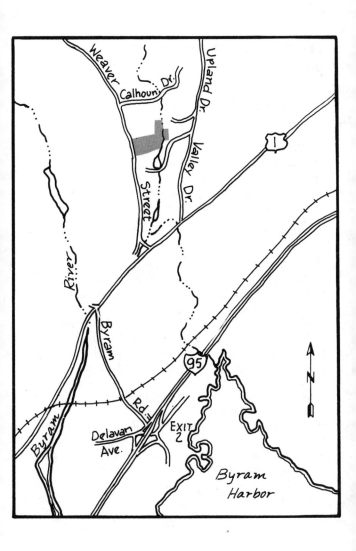

33

McKINNEY WILDLIFE REFUGE

Long Island Sound

DIRECTIONS: If you're a boater, you'll have the appropriate NOAA Charts of the Sound and will probably be quite familiar with the Norwalk Islands and Falkners Island—all accessible by sea-worthy craft. For more details, contact the U.S. Fish and Wildlife Service at 401-364-9124.

THE McKINNEY WILDLIFE REFUGE was ten years in the making and illustrates the cooperative effort of the U.S. Congress with the Conservancy and the Connecticut Audubon Society. The refuge includes Chimon Island and Sheffield Island located at Norwalk, and important nesting and feeding grounds for the herons of Long Island Sound. Falkners Island, three miles off Guilford, is a nesting ground for common and roseate terns and contains a thriving population of rabbits that, originally domestic, now are wild. The fourth component of the wildlife refuge is Milford Point—the nine-acre barrier beach stretching into the Housatonic River. The beach here provides critical nesting ground for piping plovers and least terns. In general, all areas are closed to the public from April through August due to the sensitivity of nesting birds. Management of the McKinney Wildlife Refuge is in the able hands of the U.S. Fish and Wildlife Service.

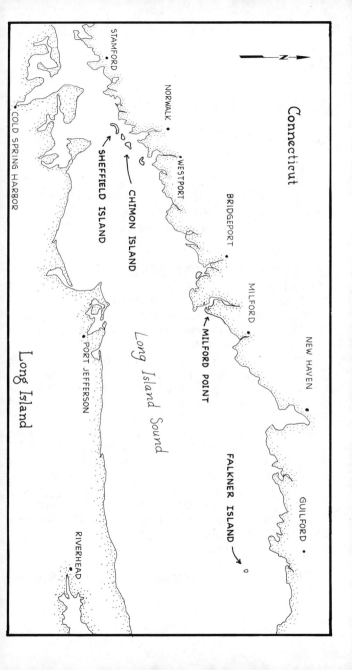

34

MESSENGER PRESERVE

Granby

DIRECTIONS: From Hartford, take Route 189 to Granby. Proceed on Route 20 to West Granby. Turn south on Simsbury Road, then immediately right on Broad Hill Road, where you can pull off and park.

THE MESSENGER PRESERVE, named after William R. and Edna S. Messenger, is 141 acres of mixed hardwoods situated in the Western Highlands of Connecticut. It has no formal trail system but is contiguous to the three-thousand–acre McLean Game Refuge where there are numerous well-marked trails.

The Messenger Preserve includes the lower south-facing slopes of Broad Hill which support a diverse canopy of black birches, maples, and red and white oaks. The dominant shrub is maple-leaved viburnum. Beach Brook flows from west to east across the central part of the preserve. The steep north face of the ravine primarily supports hemlocks. South of Messenger Road, the west-facing slope of Weed Hill supports oaks and hickories, with hemlocks and a well-developed cover of huckleberry and low blueberry.

In the past, much of the Messenger Preserve was cut over or farmed. In the late 1920s, parts of the preserve burned in a large forest fire on Broad Hill. Despite these influences, this woodland is generally more mature than the surrounding property.

Edna S. Messenger donated land for this preserve.

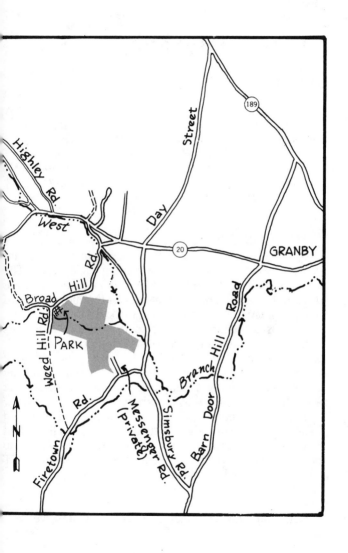

35

ORDWAY PRESERVE

Weston

DIRECTIONS: From the Merritt Parkway, take exit 42 and go north on Route 57 for 0.8 mile. Bear right on Lyons Plains Road and continue 2.5 miles. Turn left on Cart Bridge Road and right on Goodhill Road. Limited parking is provided off Goodhill Road at #165.

MUCH LIKE THE LAND of nearby Devil's Den (see chapter 9), the Ordway Preserve is underlain by resistant gneiss, which creates an undulating landscape. The topographic heights formed by this exposed bedrock are drained by several intermittent brooks that flow eastward into the East Branch of the Saugatuck River.

The eastern length of the preserve is mixed hardwoods dominated by oaks and hickories, with tulip trees and yellow birches on wetter sites. The western section is three former fields enclosed by stone walls. Two are reverting to woodland and are at different successional stages. The other has been planted as an arboretum.

The preserve is open from dawn till dusk. You are asked to register at each visit and to stay on the well-marked trails. Groups must obtain a permit prior to visiting the preserve. Write to Devil's Den, Box 1162, Weston, CT 06883, or call 203-226-4491.

Katharine Ordway donated land for this preserve.

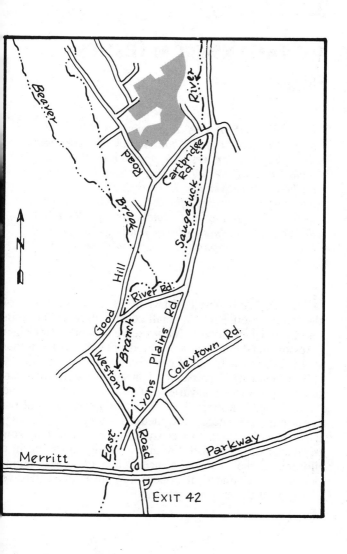

36

PATTAGANSETT MARSHES

Niantic

DIRECTIONS: Access to the marshes is by boat only. The nearest public boat launch is at the Four Mile River, on the west side opposite Rocky Neck State Park. Take exit 71 from I-95 and head south on Four Mile River Road. Turn right (west) onto Route 156 and proceed for 0.7 mile. Take a left and continue to the boat launch. Because the route to Pattagansett Marshes takes you into Long Island Sound, a small motorboat is preferable to a canoe or rowboat.

THE PATTAGANSETT MARSHES lie at the mouth of the Pattagansett River, a small coastal stream that feeds into Long Island Sound. The preserve occupies forty-eight acres of marshland and associated uplands, with another nineteen acres held under conservation easement.

The sanctuary's diverse habitats support a rich and varied flora attracting a variety of fish, invertebrates, and birds. Several nesting platforms have attracted adult osprey that have successfully fledged young. The estuary, a particularly productive ecosystem with a constant flow of nutrients, teems with life and is nicely illustrated in a diorama at the Thames Science Center in New London. Scientists at Connecticut College have also done extensive research of the marshes' ecology.

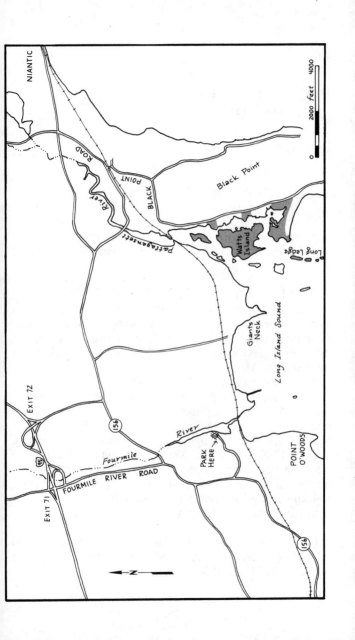

37

PIKE-MARSHALL NATURE PRESERVE

Ledyard

> *DIRECTIONS: From I-95, take exit 89 (Allyn Street). Go north on Cow Hill Road and cross Route 184 onto Pumpkin Hill Road. Go 2 miles and turn left onto Lambtown Road. Access to both preserves is on the right in 0.25 mile. See map on page 185.*

THE PIKE-MARSHALL NATURE PRESERVE is two contiguous properties, both underlain by granite gneiss with a north–south fault. The southern end of this fault causes sheer cliffs in the Pike Nature Preserve, but its northern end is buried beneath an extensive wetland in the Hugh A. Marshall Preserve.

The stone walls in the 158-acre Pike Preserve crisscross land that has reverted from farmland to mixed-hardwood forest. A variety of oaks grow on the ridgetops; the midslopes support beeches. To the east of Pumpkin Hill Road, some of the old fields have been planted in conifers.

The 112-acre Hugh A. Marshall Preserve, abutting the Pike Preserve to the north, is a wetland dominated by red maples, alders, and sweet pepperbush. The more elevated, well-drained edges support red oaks and yellow birches, with viburnum and blueberries in the shrub layer.

Dr. David Marshall and Constance Pike donated land for the core preserve. A twelve-acre addition was given by Earl and Margaret Mummert.

38

POND MOUNTAIN

Kent

DIRECTIONS: From Route 7 in Kent, take Route 341 west (across the Housatonic River and past the Kent School). Continue 1.6 miles and turn right on Macedonia Brook Road. Continue for just under one mile and take a right on Fuller Mountain Road. At the top of the hill, and just shy of one mile, turn right into the grassy parking area for Pond Mountain Natural Area.

THE NATURAL AREA AT POND MOUNTAIN comprises nearly eight hundred acres, donated by Myra H. Hopson of Kent, and administered by the Pond Mountain Trust in cooperation with The Nature Conservancy. It shares its southern boundary with St. Johns Ledges (see chapter 20), and its trail system ties in with the Appalachian Trail.

The Natural Area provides the hiker with a diverse landscape. Caleb's Peak affords splendid views of the Housatonic River Valley. Pond Mountain reaches an elevation of 1,332 feet and gives a westerly view all the way to the Catskill Mountains in New York State. Fuller Pond, a spring-fed lake, is an especially interesting feature of Pond Mountain Natural Area. Created some twelve thousand years ago as the Wisconsin Ice Cap retreated, it is exceptionally deep and clear, and has been the subject of many research projects. The broad path that rings the lake is a pretty walk in any season.

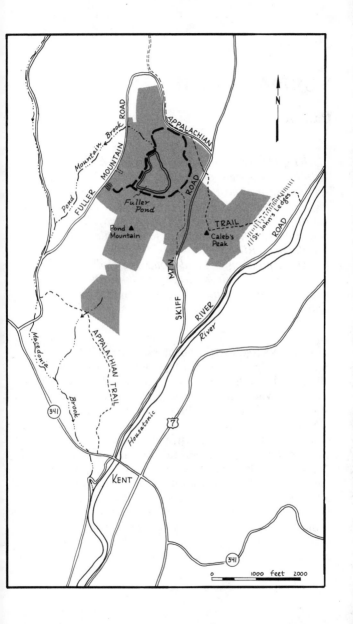

N

Pond Mountain Brook Road

FULLER MOUNTAIN BROOK ROAD

APPALACHIAN

Fuller Pond

MTN. ROAD

SKIFF

TRAIL

St. John's Ledges

Pond Mountain

Caleb's Peak

ROAD

RIVER

River

Macedonia

APPALACHIAN TRAIL

Brook

Housatonic

341

7

KENT

341

0   1000 feet   2000

39

ROBBINS SWAMP

Canaan

DIRECTIONS: From Canaan, head south on Route 7, bear right on Route 126 (Sand Road), and continue for almost 2.5 miles. Stop at the Hollenbeck River ("Point of Rocks"). From Falls Village, head north on Route 7, go left on Page Road, then right on Sand Road, and continue for 0.6 mile. Stop at the Hollenbeck River.

At the junction of Sand Road, the Hollenbeck River, and the railroad tracks, walk north along the tracks for about a mile. The huge swamp lies to the east.

ROBBINS SWAMP is the largest wetland in Connecticut, encompassing more than fifteen hundred acres in Canaan. Of this, the state owns about five hundred acres, while the Conservancy, through the generous gift of Mrs. Louise Stanton, protects over a hundred acres in three tracts.

Sand Road runs along the base of a lime-rock ridge. Once the leaves have fallen, you can readily see the limestone mines where the white rock is exposed. It is the runoff from these cliffs, as well as the limestone underlying the valley, that enriches the soils and supports a special and rare array of plant species, which includes bur oak, northern white cedar, and false melic grass. While access is difficult and there are only deer paths to follow, the preserve is included as one of the state's best examples of a calcareous fen and seepage swamp.

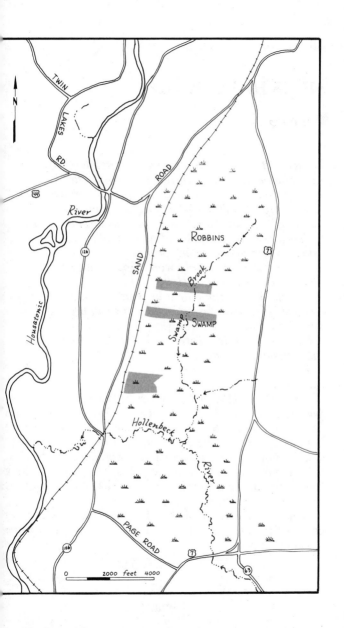

40

SILAS HALL POND

Winchester

DIRECTIONS: From Norfolk, turn south on Route 272 and go 1.5 miles. Turn left on Winchester Road, go 1.3 miles, and turn left again on Danbury Quarter Road. Go 2.2 miles and turn right (south) on Grantville Road. Park at a school-bus turnaround 1.2 miles down Grantville Road or go another 1,000 feet south where there's room for a car or two at the side of the road. Here, an old woods road leads slightly to the right down to Silas Hall Pond.

From the last traffic light in Winsted, follow Route 44 west for about 2 miles. Where a small brook crosses Route 44, go west (left) on Danbury Quarter Road for 1.6 miles. Turn south (left) on Grantville Road and go 1.4 miles.

THE 108 ACRES of the preserve, donated by Bethuel Webster, are either wet or very steep—terrain typical of the northwest corner of the state. The uplands are dominated by northern mixed hardwoods; the lower slopes support a characteristic association of hemlocks, yellow birches, and red maples. The bog that lies along the north and west shore of Silas Hall Pond has a dense growth of heath shrubs.

Beavers have invaded the area, and their dams have caused the water level to rise and flood out some of the lowland forests.

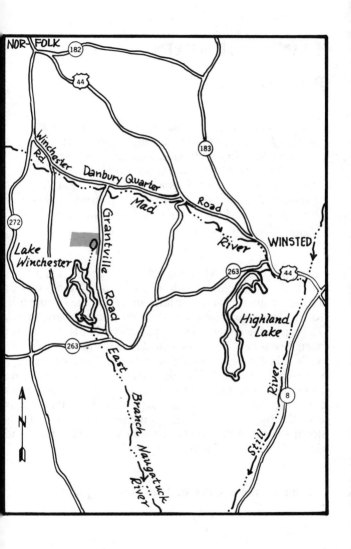

41

TAINE MOUNTAIN

Burlington

*DIRECTIONS: From Unionville, follow Route 4
west, which parallels the Farmington River. At the
blinking light, turn left and continue on Route 4
west. Take the first left south on Punch Brook
Road. Continue for 0.8 mile and turn left onto Taine
Mountain Road. Limited parking is possible at the
edge of the road where the blue-blazed trail intersects
Taine Mountain Road.*

TAINE MOUNTAIN, underlain by gneiss and till, is
situated on the eastern side of the Bristol dome, one of
a series of gneiss domes, or hills, that flank the Farmington
River. The entire area was once cleared for agriculture.
The top of the mountain was partially orchards and has not
been developed. Enormous shade trees still line the stone
walls. Chestnut oaks dominate the ridge, from which there
is a view to the west. The Blue Trail leads south off Taine
Mountain Road and continues a short distance to Perry's
Lookout. You may continue farther south on the trail or
take the fork back to Taine Mountain Road, which leads
down an old logging road filled with hay-scented ferns and
flanked by oaks, maples, ashes, and hickories.

John S. Dunning donated land for this preserve.

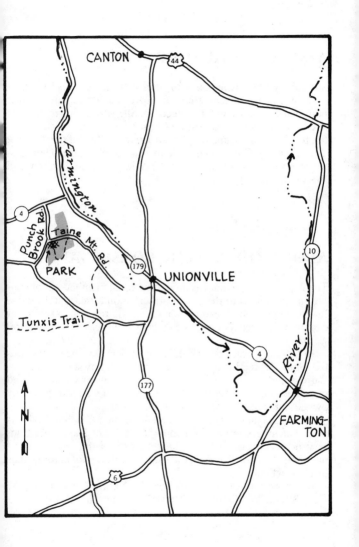

CANTON

44

Farmington

4

Punch Brook Rd.

Taine Mt. Rd.

PARK

179

UNIONVILLE

Tunxis Trail

4

River

10

N

177

FARMING-TON

6

ABOUT THE AUTHOR

Susan D. Cooley is the director of investment services for Farm-vest, Inc., a farm-preservation/land-investment company based at Folly Farm in Simsbury, Connecticut. She was associate director and land steward of The Nature Conservancy, Connecticut Chapter, for seven years, and remains an active member of the Board of Trustees of the Connecticut Chapter. Ms. Cooley earned her Master of Forest Science degree at the Yale School of Forestry and Environmental Studies.

ABOUT THE NATURE CONSERVANCY

The Nature Conservancy is an international membership organization committed to the global preservation of natural diversity. Its mission is to find, protect, and maintain the best examples of communities, ecosystems, and endangered species in the natural world.

To date, the Conservancy and its members have been responsible for the protection of 3,285,134 acres in all fifty states, Canada, Latin America, and the Caribbean. The Conservancy owns and manages about a thousand preserves—the largest privately owned nature-preserve system in the world.

More than 440,000 individual members and four hundred corporate members nationwide support the work of The Nature Conservancy. The Connecticut Chapter, with its thirteen thousand members, has saved over eighteen thousand acres of natural lands in Connecticut.

For more information write to: The Nature Conservancy, 55 High Street, Middletown, CT 06457, or call (203) 344–0716.